CREATED BY GOD

Created by God: About Human Sexuality for Older Girls and Boys (ISBN-0-687-75345-7).

Student Book

An official resource for The United Methodist Church prepared by the General Board of Discipleship through the Division of Church School Publications and published by Graded Press, a division of The United Methodist Publishing House, 201 Eighth Avenue, South, P.O. Box 801, Nashville, TN 37202. Printed in the United States of America.

Scripture quotations in this publication, unless otherwise identified, are from the *Good News Bible: The Bible in Today's English Version*. Old Testament: Copyright American Bible Society 1976; New Testament: Copyright American Bible Society 1966, 1971, 1976. Used by permission.

For permission to reproduce any material in this publication, call 615-749-6421, or write to Graded Press, Syndication-Permissions Office, 201 Eighth Avenue, South, P.O. Box 801, Nashville, TN 37202.

To order copies of this publication, call toll free: 800-672-1789. Call Monday through Friday from 8:00-4:00 Central Time or 8:30-4:30 Pacific Time. Use your Cokesbury account, American Express, Visa, Discover, or MasterCard.

Editorial Team
James H. Ritchie, Jr., Editor
E. Michael Fleenor, Assistant Editor
Crystal Zinkiewicz, Product Developer

Design Team
Adolph C. Lavin, Design Supervisor
Bob Finney, Layout Designer

Administrative Staff
H. Claude Young, Jr., Editor of Church School Publications
M. Franklin Dotts, Executive Editor of Children's Publications

CREATED BY GOD

ABOUT HUMAN SEXUALITY
FOR OLDER GIRLS AND BOYS

by Dorlis Brown Glass

with James H. Ritchie, Jr.

Illustrated by Doug Jones and Tom Armstrong

Dear New Friend,

My name is Dorlis Glass. My husband Verne and I have been married for more than thirty-five years. Our three children are grown—all with their own families. Our six grandchildren range in age from infant twins to a teenager.

I've worked for many years with boys and girls your age in Sunday school, summer camp, and as a writer. Ten years ago I helped to create a study for fifth and sixth graders called *God Made Me: About Sex and Growing Up*. Around that same time I began leading human sexuality workshops for young people and their parents.

At first I was nervous. I worried about questions that might be asked during the workshops and wondered how I would answer them. My worrying and wondering started me thinking about some of the girls and boys I know and love and about what *they* expect from adults.

Young people expect adults to *respect* them—to listen, take questions seriously, and be honest. I decided that if I didn't know the answer to a question, I would say, "I don't know. Let's find out." I'm thankful when this happens, for in looking together for answers, we all learn and grow.

I am not a parenting expert, the perfect parent, or the parent of perfect children. If I were starting over, I'd do some things differently. Some things I'd do pretty much the same. Anyway, our three children have grown to be persons we respect. Each is special and loved. So are *you*!

Through my children, grandchildren, and the young people with whom I work, I've gained a fairly good sense of what *you're* going through. As you read and reread this book, you and I will be celebrating two of God's gifts to you. One is your sexuality. The other is the people who love you and try to help you better understand this wonderful part of yourself.

Affectionately,

Dorlis Brown Glass

Contents

Chapter 1

A Growing, Changing, Child of God

Today we celebrate YOU and this special time in your life. You're growing and changing. You're being challenged by new ideas and new responsibilities. You're dreaming and making plans. You have a whole new set of questions, concerns, and even some fears.

God's design calls for growth and change. Sometimes change happens gently—like the blooming of a flower. Sometimes it sneaks up with the suddenness of an unexpected snow storm! Whether by bloom, blizzard, or something in-between, change is happening to *you*. It's a confusing but wonderful time. Frightening and frustrating as change can be, it does have a place in God's plan for you. You, my friend, are a growing, changing, child of God.

One Very Special Young Person

We have only one glimpse of Jesus between the time he was a baby and the time he was an adult. That glimpse is of a time when he was about your age. Like you, Jesus was growing and changing.

Have you ever wondered how Jesus felt as he was growing up? what he liked to do? what he worried about? who his friends were? what they did together? if he was ever afraid? if he got bored with chores he was expected to do? Do you think he ever spent time daydreaming as you do? What were his hopes for the future? What might have helped him know that he was maturing as a person and as God's child?

A Son of the Law

"Hurry, Son!" called Joseph from the doorway of the carpenter's shop. "The caravan will be leaving Nazareth soon. Come help load supplies on the donkeys."

A short time later, Jesus and his parents, together with other Jewish pilgrims, started south toward Jerusalem. Yes, they had been making this annual Passover journey for years, but this time it would be different. Mary and Joseph had been thinking about, talking about, and planning for this trip since the day Jesus was born. Though at twelve he still had lots of growing to do, Jesus was now considered an adult according to Jewish tradition—a *bar mitzvah*—"son of command" or "son of the Law." Jesus would have new responsibilities and new privileges. He was expected to make wise choices. This visit to the Temple would be a celebration of his growing up.

The caravan was accompanied by the jingle of camel bells, the bray of donkeys, and the laughter of children. The days went by quickly. Soon the company of pilgrims began to make its way along the narrow, twisting road from Jericho to Jerusalem. Midway between the cities they made camp near an inn. While the adults exchanged news and stories around the campfires, the children chattered on about the beautiful Temple and the marvelous city they would be visiting.

"I was born in Bethlehem—just a few miles from Jerusalem," Jesus told his friends. "When I was eight days old, my parents took me to the Temple and dedicated me to God." The others joined in with stories that had been told about *their* dedications, shared memories of earlier trips to Jerusalem, and told of their plans for this Passover adventure.

At first light, they broke camp and started out on the last leg of their journey. Rounding a bend in the road, Jesus looked up at the massive walls and great watchtowers of Jerusalem that overlooked the roads and valleys below. His heart pounded with anticipation. He and Joseph had talked many times about this trip. The pictures in his mind were clear. He knew that the experience would be an unforgettable one. Eagerly, Jesus and his friends ran ahead, reaching the city gate before the others. Dancing impatiently, they awaited the arrival of the rest of the caravan.

For the next several days, Jesus explored the city. Every day he visited the Temple, where he watched the sacrifices being offered to God—one of the privileges of being considered an adult. A full participant now in the Temple worship, he listened eagerly as the teachers read and explained the meaning of God's Law. Though he had often heard many of the words before, he found that he was able to understand them in new and exciting ways.

The days in Jerusalem were full, and all too soon the Passover came to a close. On the day they left to return to Nazareth, the women and children, generally moving more slowly, departed earlier than the men. As Mary made one last check to be sure that everything had been packed on the donkeys, she wondered why Jesus wasn't there to help. With a smile she remembered; and as the caravan began to move, she sighed and said to herself, "How quickly things change! Last year Jesus was here at my side. Now he is a bar mitzvah and travels with his father and the rest of the men.

I'm sure that my grown-up son will have many stories to tell at the fire this evening!"

As Joseph and the other men prepared to leave the city, he assumed that Jesus was traveling with his mother, just as he had always done. "My son," he chuckled to himself, "an adult!" Joseph knew the tradition of his people, but he also knew that Jesus was at that awkward age—no longer a child and not yet an adult.

As evening came, the men caught up with the women and together they began to prepare the campsite. Mary and Joseph realized for the first time that Jesus was not with either of them. Anxiously they moved through the caravan, stopping at the tents and cooking fires of friends and family to ask if anyone had seen Jesus. Convinced that Jesus was not with the caravan, they hurriedly collected their things and headed back toward Jerusalem.

For three days they searched the city. Jesus was nowhere to be found. On the fourth day they thought to look in the Temple. There he was! Seated at the feet of the teachers, Jesus was listening carefully to their words. There was so much to absorb—how would he ever take it all in? The teachers were amazed by the understanding reflected in the questions he asked.

Feelings of relief flooded over Joseph and Mary as they realized that Jesus was safe—feelings that quickly turned to bewilderment as to why Jesus would do such a thing. Jesus saw the worry on his parents' faces and heard the fear in their voices. "Didn't you know that I had to be in my Father's house?" Jesus asked, sounding surprised that his parents didn't know where he would be. They *hadn't* known, and they *didn't* understand all of the changes that were taking place in their son. This was not the last time that they would be puzzled by Jesus' behavior. For now, Mary would tuck this incident away in her mind. Someday, perhaps, she *would* understand.

Joseph, Mary, and Jesus made the journey back to Nazareth together. At times they talked and at times they were silent—unable to find words to express the feelings they had about the changes that affected not only Jesus but their whole family. The story ends with these words: "Jesus grew both in body and in wisdom, gaining favor with God and others" (Luke 2:41-52, adapted).

Jesus was traveling through *adolescence
(a-doh-LES-sens)—the period between childhood and
adulthood. Like you, he was growing, wondering, testing,
and discovering. While his family remained important to him,
he was developing relationships outside his family. Where
once he contented himself to play on the floor of his father's
carpenter shop, drawing pictures in the sawdust and building
towers with scraps of wood, he now worked and learned at
his father's side—lifting, measuring, sawing, and carving. He
no longer had the body of a child. New muscles and new
coordination helped Jesus take on new responsibilities.

You Too Have a Growing Body

Think about how *you* have grown and changed in the past
few years. That baldheaded little person pictured in the
family photo album was *you* not so long ago. On the
following page of the album might be a picture of a crying
toddler, showing grandpa a skinned elbow or knee. Then
there's the one of your first day of school, of your first dance
recital, of you in your scout uniform, or of you in the
children's program at church. How you've grown! Wasn't it
just the other day that your mom or dad mentioned how
many jeans sizes you've gone through this past year?

Have you wondered, *Am I supposed to be growing this
fast? Should I be growing faster? Do other kids feel as
awkward as I do? Am I weird?*

Your body is changing in ways other than size. In fact, it
could very well be that you *haven't* noticed much difference.

---

*The words you see printed in **dark type** are also found in the glossary located in the back
of the book. The words you might have difficulty pronouncing are accompanied by a
pronunciation guide. Accent the capitalized syllable.

in your height or weight. That's perfectly OK. But change *is* happening. The shape of your body is changing. Your energy levels are changing—one moment you've got energy to spare, and the next you're so tired you could drop. With physical changes come changes in mood. You find yourself suddenly shifting from laughing happily with your friends to shouting at them as though they were long-time enemies. Confused parents just shake their heads. If only they knew the confusion *you* feel at times!

Do you suppose that Jesus felt this way too?

Growing in Wisdom

Jesus was growing wiser. You might wonder, *Does that mean he didn't know everything from the very beginning?* No, he didn't. He grew up just as I did and just as you are doing. As his body matured, so did his mind. He grew in his ability to make choices based on what he knew and on how his decisions would affect others. He was learning to live responsibly.

You're trying to live responsibly too. You're becoming aware that what you do affects many people. You're more aware of the homeless, of people who haven't adequate food or medical care. You may be wondering what you can do to help. You ask questions and look for solutions, but you sometimes feel frustrated because adults don't seem to take you seriously. You get angry when you see people treated unfairly, and you want want to correct such situations. But how?

At times you find yourself questioning things you've always believed to be true. You ask, *Is it all right to doubt?* You feel impatient when others expect you to think as they do or expect you to think as you have always thought in the past. Sometimes you're impatient with people who keep telling you to grow up when you're not convinced that you're *ready* to give up the *child* part of yourself. You may be discovering

that when you disagree with the way things have always been, people get upset. Jesus certainly discovered that the changes taking place in *him* were disrupting the lives of his parents!

Deep down, *you* know what Jesus knew. Asking questions and acting on your own discoveries is important. You are learning to set goals for yourself. You are preparing for the future. Setting goals is a difficult but important part of growing in wisdom.

Gaining Favor With God and Others

The way you feel about others may be changing too. You want to share your dreams with the people who are important to you. Then again, you want privacy—quiet times in which to explore your dreams. You want to be more independent, to take greater control of your life; but not everyone is ready to allow you that independence. The truth is, even *you* may question how ready you are to become more independent.

Confused? Who wouldn't be! A friend once said of her son, "One day Doug was twelve going on twenty. The next, he was twelve going on six!" Does Doug sound at all like you? The ups and downs leave you feeling like you're on a roller coaster. I remember feeling that way myself.

Growing Up Takes Time

Growing up can't be rushed. It takes time for bodies to grow and develop. It takes time for us to learn through study and experience to make responsible decisions. It takes time for us to learn how to live with others in Christlike love and respect.

Sometimes nature points us to answers. In our front yard is a large pecan tree. Each autumn, as cool winds begin to blow and nights turn chilly, the outer coverings on the pecans start to open. After several weeks the wind blows colder and harder, and the pecans fall. We scurry to gather the nuts before the squirrels hide all of them.

I remember the first autumn in our house. *Surely I can hurry things along*, I thought impatiently. I shook the limbs of the pecan tree and whacked at them with a broom, only to find that the still-green coverings of the nuts I had knocked down were holding still-green pecans tight inside. I'll bet the squirrels (and the neighbors) were amused by my antics!

We must wait. In God's own time, the Holy Spirit—the Giver of life—will deliver God's gift of maturity, just as the wind delivers the nuts from the pecan tree. Nine months you waited in your mother's womb to be born. Now you wait to get started with, to get on with, or to get finished with a period of growth as dramatic as that spent in the warm quietness of the womb. You wait and wonder. You grow and mature. Just as the pecans mature in their own time, you are maturing into a very special person.

Like a Diamond

One of earth's precious gems is the diamond. A diamond is a piece of carbon—the same principle element found in a piece of coal. This chunk of carbon doesn't start out beautiful. The original stone, taken from the ground, doesn't sparkle. It takes the skilled eye of the miner to see the potential beauty in the stone. It takes the skilled hands of the cutter to give it its many surfaces. These surfaces or facets catch and reflect the light, giving the diamond its beauty and value.

In some ways, you are like that diamond. You are interesting, special, and valuable because there are many facets to who you are. Your unique combination of qualities

makes you different and distinct from all other people. Some of your facets are. . .

your age;
your size and shape;
your skin, eye, and hair colors;
your **gender** (being female or being male);
your interests and abilities;
your likes and dislikes;
your relationships; and
your place within the family.

Your Special Place in a Family

One day, some young friends and I were talking about families. I asked them, "What *is* a family?" Some of their answers were:

A family is a group of people who are related to one another.

A family cares about one another.

A family helps one another.

A family laughs with you when you're happy and cries with you when you're sad.

A family usually lives together—then again, they don't always.

My friends' answers sometimes described how their families look. We discovered that families are as different as individual persons. Some families had two parents; some had one. Some families had one child; others had more. Some were blended families with children who had been born to one of the parents but not to both. Some were "birth" families; others were adopted families. There were families with grandparents, cousins, aunts, and uncles living together. One child lived in a foster family—a family that cares for children who are not related to that family by birth or by legal adoption. All were families, regardless of how well they fit the traditional idea of what it takes to be a family.

Families Change as You Change

When you were a baby, people cared for all of your needs. As you have grown older, you have been more and more capable of taking care of yourself. Now you are in the process of learning to care for others. As you have grown and changed, so has your family. That's an important idea for you to think about. Families aren't names; they aren't addresses; they aren't houses. Families are people. People change, so families change. You sometimes wish that everything else in your life would stay exactly the same while you are going through this time of change. After all, enough is enough!

That wish is understandable, but it won't happen. And you really wouldn't want it to. Change means that parents begin to trust you to do things that you weren't allowed to do when you were younger: spending the day shopping downtown or at a mall with a friend, doing some babysitting for neighbors or finding other ways to earn personal spending money. Change also means new limitations. Some of the actions that were acceptable from you as a child are no longer appropriate. Now that you are moving toward adulthood, you can say with the apostle Paul, "I have no more use for childish ways" (1 Corinthians 13:11). Families are an important part of discovering what is appropriate and what isn't. As you and your family grow and change together, you will be making such discoveries.

Belonging to God's Family

All of us have one thing in common. We were each created in the image of God. You've heard people say something like, "Jessie is the spitting *image* of her mother!" They are saying that either in her appearance or in her actions, Jessie is much like her mother. You and I were created by *God*. We were created in the *image* of God—

created **like** God (Genesis 1:26-27). What is there about us that identifies us as belonging to God's family and therefore being like God?

Like God, you have a hand in the creation of something new—the new person you are becoming. Many of the changes you are experiencing and will experience are factors over which you have no control. Others will call for decisions on your part. Most of these decisions involve your relationships with other people. The decisions you make will, in part, help to shape the person you will become. You, God, your family, and the other significant people in your life share that important task.

"Jesus grew both in body and in wisdom, gaining favor with God and others." The same thing is happening to you. You are a growing, changing, child of God!

Chapter 2

Inside and Out: How Change Comes About

Oh what a wonderful, marvelous, glorious,
What a fantastic creation we are!
When I look all around I am reminded
We're far more amazing than earth, sea, and star![1]

"Oh, I already know all that stuff!" said Brenda to a friend when she heard that her church was planning a study on human sexuality. "Me, too!" said the friend.

Maybe *you're* saying the same thing. After all, you and your friends talk some (and maybe giggle some) about sex. You discuss it every once in a while with a parent or another adult. You have an older brother or sister who answers your questions from time to time. You've read a book on the subject, or you've seen THE FILM about sex that is shown at school once you reach a certain grade. So, let's agree that you already know some important stuff about how your body functions.

While most girls know something about what's happening to girls' bodies, and most boys know something about what's happening to boys' bodies, most girls don't know much about boys, and boys aren't very well-informed about girls. So, here's a chance to see the whole picture!

The Chicken or the Egg?

Where *is* the best place to begin? Do we start with the chicken or the egg? My five-year-old friend Suzie was spending the night with her grandparents when the subject came up.

"Grandma, did you know baby chickens come out of eggs?"

"Yes, chickens and turkeys, ducks and birds come out of eggs."

"And *people*!"

"No, *chickens* and *turkeys* and *ducks* and *birds* come out of eggs."

"And *some* people!"

"No, Honey. Chickens and ducks and birds come out of eggs, but people don't."

There was a long, thoughtful pause.

"Are you sure?"

"Yes, I'm sure."

How did Suzie get so confused? Her Aunt Kim had recently given birth, and she had talked at length with Suzie about the pregnancy and about the arrival of the new cousin.

"Do you remember when Aunt Kim went to the hospital to have her baby?"

"Yes, but I thought she went to the hospital to lay her egg!"

Suzie was only five and hadn't pieced the story together correctly, but she was getting close. Sometimes we're a bit like Suzie, needing only a little more information in order to better understand.

In the Beginning

In the beginning . . . God created human beings, making them to be like God. God created them male and female, blessed them, and said, "Have many children, so that your descendants will live all over the earth and bring it under their control." . . . God looked at everything God had made and was very pleased.

Genesis 1:1, 27-28, and 31 (adapted)

Our story of human growth and development begins with neither chicken nor egg but with God. The Creation story we read in the first two chapters of Genesis tells about the beginning of life. The most important information tells us *who* was responsible, answering the question, *Who did it?*

God was responsible. We are part of God's creation and a valuable part of God's plan. What does it mean to be made *like God*? It means that we have within us the ability to *create*—to create beauty, to create peace, to create loving relationships, and even to create new life. For the creation of new life, God made us male and female. This kind of creating calls for the cooperation of people who are different from each other in many important ways. The fact that God created two different genders of human beings reminds us that we *need* each other.

Becoming Adult

Changes are taking place in your body right now—some of them seen and some of them unseen. These changes are preparing you to fully realize the joy that God has planned for people to experience with their bodies. Think about how good it feels to stretch when you get out of bed in the morning. Thank God for that feeling! As you grow, you become more coordinated. Your body is able to move in ways that help you with such things as athletics and dancing. The cooperation of body parts that comes with growing up is another gift of God.

As you grow and develop, you are becoming aware of how good it feels when someone you care about gives you a hug to say, "I love you," touches you gently when you're upset, or pats you on the back when you've done something well. Becoming an adult means getting better at caring for people through kind touches and kind words.

Finally, the changes that are going on inside and out are preparing you for the possibility that one day you may become a parent.

What a Fantastic Creation We Are!

Next let's go on a quick tour of the female and male bodies. I think you'll find it helpful to know the proper names for those body parts that make us uniquely male or female. You'll also want to know how those parts work.

The Fantastic Female

Let's start with the parts we can see. The word **genitals** (JEN-uh-tuhls), or **genitalia** (jen-uh-TAIL-yuh), refers to the external (on the outside of the body) sex organs of both females and males. **Vulva** (VUL-vuh) is the name for the female genitals, located between the legs. The vulva includes several separate structures. The **outer** or **major labia** (LAY-bee-uh) or **lips** are two thick folds of skin that surround the opening of the **vagina** (vuh-JIE-nuh). A second set of folds of skin, the **inner** or **minor labia**, are inside and sometimes hidden by the outer labia. The **clitoris** (KLIT-uh-ris) is a small cylinder-shaped organ that, in grown women, is about the size of the eraser on a pencil. Made of very sensitive tissue, the clitoris is located at the top of the inner labia. It is covered by a small hood of skin that girls need to gently pull back when cleansing the genital area. The small opening to the **urethra** (yoo-REE-thruh), which is the narrow tube that allows urine to pass from the bladder outside the body, is also part of the vulva. The urethra is totally separate from the vagina.

Just inside the opening of the vagina is a thin layer of tissue called the **hymen** (HI-muhn). This layer of tissue may be torn during some athletic activity or stretching movement

TOUR THE BODY!

The Female Reproductive System

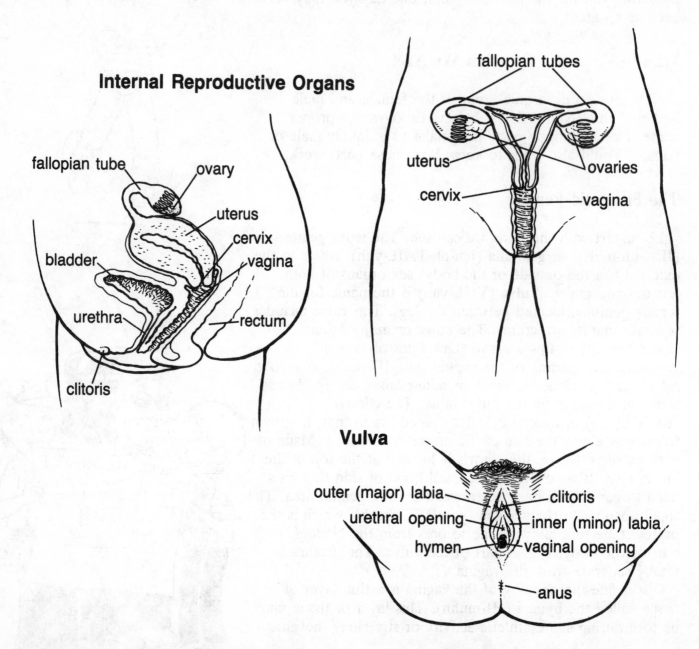

Internal Reproductive Organs

fallopian tube
ovary
uterus
cervix
vagina
bladder
urethra
rectum
clitoris

fallopian tubes
uterus
ovaries
cervix
vagina

Vulva

outer (major) labia
urethral opening
hymen
clitoris
inner (minor) labia
vaginal opening
anus

or during the first experience of **sexual intercourse**. Some women are born without a hymen. The **anus** (AY-nuhs), the opening where solid waste leaves the body, is not part of the vulva, but is located in the same general area.

Now we move to the internal sex organs. The vagina, which I've already mentioned, is an elastic, muscular passageway connecting the lower end of the **uterus** (YOO-tuhr-us) to the outside of the body. The vagina is not large—three to four inches long when fully developed—but can stretch to receive the erect male **penis** (PEE-nuhs) during sexual intercourse or to allow a baby to travel out of the mother's body during childbirth. The uterus, or **womb** (WOOM), is a hollow organ located inside the lower abdomen and is shaped like a lightbulb or an upside-down pear. It is usually no bigger than a closed fist, but during **pregnancy** (PREG-nun-see) it stretches to accommodate the baby growing inside.

The **fallopian** (fa-LOH-pee-uhn) **tubes** branch out from either side of the upper part of the uterus. At the end of the tubes are the **ovaries** (OH-vuh-reez), two almond-sized organs located a little lower than the waist. Stored in the ovaries are thousands of **ova** (OH-vuh), or female reproductive cells. The ovaries also produce female **hormones** (HOR-mohns) which will be mentioned later.

The Marvelous Male

The male genitals have two main parts. The first is the penis, the cylinder-shaped organ that gets called everything but a penis. The cylinder part of the penis is called the **shaft**. The end or head of the penis is called the **glans** (GLANZ) and, like the clitoris in the female, is the most sensitive part of the male genitals.

The shaft of the penis is covered with a loose layer of skin. Male babies are born with a **foreskin** (FOR-skin)—the portion of this layer of skin that extends down over the

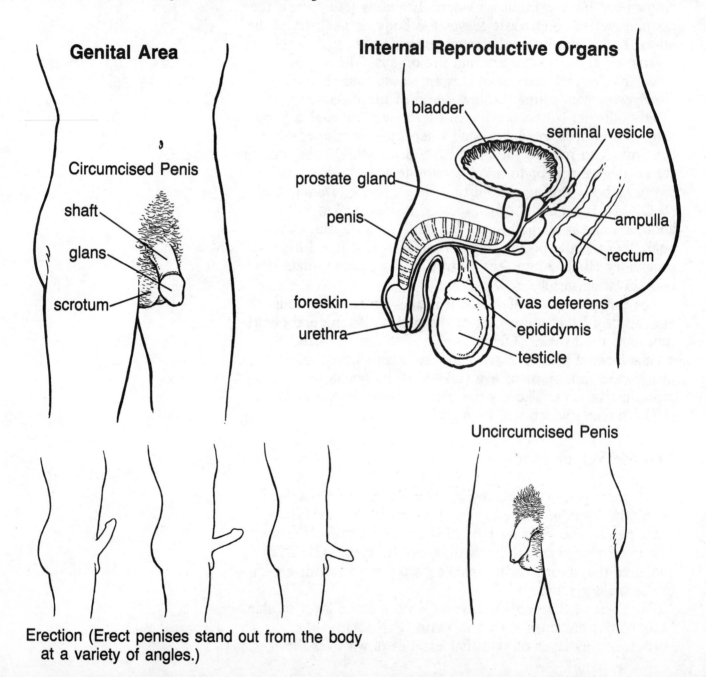

The Male Reproductive System

Erection (Erect penises stand out from the body
at a variety of angles.)

glans. Sometimes an operation called **circumcision** (sir-cum-SIZH-un), in which a doctor removes the foreskin, is performed shortly after birth.

Circumcision, for some people, is a religious custom. Perhaps you first heard or read the word *circumcision* in the Bible. For the Hebrew people, circumcision is an important symbol. It is one way by which a boy or man is identified as a Jew. It symbolizes belonging to the people who have entered into a covenant, a special relationship, with God.

Many parents continue to have their sons **circumcised** (SIR-cum-sized) because it has been the traditional practice in their families. However, doctors no longer recommend this procedure and, as a result, more parents today are choosing *not* to have their sons circumcised. While an uncircumcised male *does* need to pull his foreskin back and clean under it when he bathes or showers, there is no known advantage to being circumcised. Occasionally, a boy or man who was not circumcised in infancy will find that his foreskin is unusually tight and difficult to pull back. In such a case circumcision may be necessary.

At the center of the glans is the opening to the urethra, which, as in the female, is the tube that allows urine to drain from the bladder. In males, however, the urethra is also part of the reproductive system.

The second main part of the male genitals is the **scrotum** (SKRO-tum), the pouch of skin that is located beneath the penis. Inside the scrotum are the two **testicles** (TESS-tih-kuhls) or **testes** (TESS-tees), egg-shaped organs in which the male reproductive cells or **sperm** and male hormones are produced. Attached to each testicle is a small muscle that acts as a thermostat, keeping the testicles at the proper temperature for the production of sperm. Cold causes the muscle to draw the testicles up to keep them warm; heat causes the muscle to relax, allowing the testicles to hang away from the body.

Particularly after the testicles have begun to grow, most boys find that one testicle—usually the left—will hang lower than the other. This is the body's way of protecting two very sensitive organs from being painfully pressed together between the legs, particularly when boys or men are being very active. The athletic supporters (jock straps) or cup protectors that boys and men wear when involved in athletics are another way of protecting the testicles, holding them close to the body.

After sperm are produced in the testicles, the sperm travel to the **epididymis** (ep-uh-DID-uh-mis), a mass of tiny tubes attached to the back of each testicle. The sperm mature during the four to six weeks it takes for them to move through the epididymis. Leading up from the epididymis is a **vas deferens** (VAZ DEHF-uhr-uhnz) or **sperm duct**. The vas deferens is a tube that loops up over the bladder and connects the testicle to the **ampulla** (am-POOL-uh)—the widened portion at the end of the vas deferens that serves as the sperm storage area. At the lower part of the ampulla, the **seminal vesicles** (SEM-uh-nuhl VESS-ih-kuhls) connect to the sperm duct. The seminal vesicles make the whitish fluid called **semen** (SEE-muhn). This semen, as we will see later, is critical to the reproductive process.

One more organ, and we'll have completed the tour. The **prostate** (PROSS-tate) **gland** is located beneath the bladder, at the intersection of the ampulla and seminal vesicles. In addition to making fluid that is added to the semen, the prostate is responsible for the squeezing action or **ejaculation** (ee-jack-yoo-LAY-shun) that pushes the sperm and semen through the urethra and out of the body.

To Everything a Time

Everything that happens in this world happens at the time God chooses.

Ecclesiastes 3:1

"What determines when I will start to grow and change, how quickly that will happen, and when it will all be over?"

"How will I know if I am *normal*?"

Normal is not a particularly helpful idea. We can talk about *averages*. If Roslyn has her first **period** when she is eleven, and Lucy has her first when she is fifteen, the *average* of the two is thirteen. But which one is *normal*? If Gary starts shaving when he is eighteen, and Russ starts when he is fourteen, which of *them* is normal? NOW HEAR THIS! *All* of them are normal, and so are *you*! *Normal* is what is right for *you*.

Within every cell of your body are **genes**—structures that determine what qualities you inherited from your parents, from their parents, and so forth. Among other physical characteristics, genes determine when you will start and how quickly you will go through **puberty** (PEW-bur-tee). Puberty refers to that time in your life when your body is changing from that of a child to that of an adult. Looking at members of your family—brothers, sisters, and cousins—you might make a guess as to when and how fast you will mature. You can also look around at people who might be your age or a bit older and guess what you have to look forward to. But remember, these are only guesses! Regardless of how quickly or how slowly the members of your family or other people your age matured or are maturing, you will still move along at the pace that is right for you.

She bodies, he bodies—each one unique;
Every conceivable size and physique.
Your's is the special one God had in mind!
Look in the mirror and there you will find:
Oh what a wonderful, marvelous, glorious,
What a fantastic creation we are!
When I look all around, I am reminded
We're far more amazing than earth, sea, and star![1]

Inside your brain is a tiny organ called the **pituitary gland** (pih-TOO-uh-tare-ee). A few years before one notices the signs of puberty, the pituitary gland begins sending substances called hormones to the ovaries in the female and to the testicles in the male. The reproductive glands (ovaries and testicles) respond to the hormone signals from the pituitary gland by producing hormones of their own.

A Closer Look at Being a Girl

As girls grow older, the pituitary gland produces larger amounts of hormones, causing the ovaries to make increasing amounts of the female hormone **estrogen** (ESS-truh-juhn). The illustrations on pages 39, 40, and 41 show five girls at eleven, sixteen, and twenty-one years old. Estrogen is responsible for all of the changes that you see taking place as the girls grow older—changes such as the following:

- A growth spurt. This will put many girls ahead of the boys their age in terms of height. Girls generally begin their time of faster growth about two years before the boys.
- The growth of **pubic** (PEW-bick) hair (the curly hairs growing in the genital area).
- The darkening and growth of hair on the legs.
- The growth of hair in the underarms.
- The darker, thicker, and more wrinkly appearance of the outer and inner labia.
- The increased sensitivity of the genital area. As puberty begins, girls discover new sensations as they explore the vaginal (VA-juh-nuhl) area and the clitoris. The touching or stroking of the genitals is part of the self-discovery process of all boys and girls. This kind of touching is called **masturbation** (mass-ter-BAY-shun). As puberty begins, girls find that the *nice* feelings they had as young children while handling their genitals have been replaced by much stronger feelings. In response to sexual stimulation, there is an increase in the amount of blood flowing to the genital area, causing the clitoris to become larger or erect. At puberty, masturbation may lead to the intense and pleasant pulsing of muscles called an **orgasm** (OR-gaz-uhm). More will be said about masturbation in chapter 4.

- The thickening of the hymen.
- The sensitivity and development of the **breasts**.
- The widening of the hips and general change in body shape.
- The growth of the uterus. It still doesn't get very large, but the walls become thicker.
- The beginning of **menstruation** (men-STRAY-shun).

A New Function; a New Rhythm

A cycle is something that happens again and again. Like the beat to your favorite song, the female body has its own rhythm or cycle. The estrogen produced by the ovaries signals the body when it's time to "catch the beat." The signal comes most often between the ages of ten and fifteen, but can come earlier or later.

At this point, the ova or reproductive cells in the ovaries begin to change and mature, or ripen. One of these ova leaves one of the ovaries about once a month. At the same time, the inner wall of the uterus is covered with a thick carpet-like lining. If the **ovum** (OH-vuhm)—the singular of ova—leaving the ovary is fertilized by a sperm cell from a male, the ovum implants in the carpet. The carpet-like lining and the ovum then form a **placenta** (pluh-SEN-tuh), which supplies nutrition to the developing infant during pregnancy.

Obviously, girls and women do not become pregnant every month. When the ovum is not fertilized, the body tells itself, *There's no fertilized ovum in here, no fetus needing a place to grow, so I don't need this extra lining in my uterus.* So, a couple of weeks after **ovulation** (ah-vue-LAY-shun), which is the release of the ovum, the uterus sheds its lining as a bloody discharge that passes from the body by way of the vagina. This process is menstruation, often referred to as the **menstrual** (MEN-struhl) **period**. The length of the period varies from person to person, but usually lasts from four to seven days.

During menstruation, a girl or woman protects her clothing by using a feminine hygiene product—either a cotton-like pad called a **sanitary napkin**, or a small, tightly-wrapped cylinder of cotton-like material called a **tampon** (TAM-pahn). The sanitary napkin or pad is fastened to the inside of the panties by adhesive strips and covers the vulva. The tampon is inserted into the vagina. Both items absorb the menstrual discharge and are replaced as needed. As menstrual flow subsides, many girls and women wear a thin panty liner or light day's pad with a bottom layer of plastic. This extra precaution insures protection should there be a continued light discharge.

Bathing and washing are especially important during menstruation. Many girls and women find that they perspire more at this time and that their perspiration has a stronger odor. Bathing frequently and paying particular attention to the genital area, the use of a deodorant or antiperspirant under the arms, and regular changing of the pad or tampon generally lessen the problem.

Girls usually have little difficulty with menstruation. They can bathe, take part in sports, and continue their normal activities. Some girls, however, may experience abdominal cramping, pain in the legs or back, or headaches. An aspirin substitute such as ibuprofen or acetomenophen usually relieves the temporary discomfort, as does the use of a heating pad. If she experiences a lot of discomfort, a girl should ask the advice of her physician.

Although the menstrual period generally occurs monthly, *monthly* refers to an approximate length of time. The cycle

might repeat every twenty-seven or twenty-eight days but could take longer. Normal is whatever is experienced by the individual girl or woman. Sometimes girls have irregular mentrual periods for the first few cycles or even the first two or three years after menstruation begins.

Menstruation is normal, but it's not always convenient! Because it is difficult to know exactly when the menstrual period will start, many girls prepare by keeping a sanitary pad or tampon in their purses or school lockers. Rest rooms and school nurses' offices often have a supply available as well.

One day a girl your age asked me, "What do you do if you start your period while you're at school and your teacher's a man?" I told her that male teachers, as well as females, understand that menstruation is a part of every girl's life. A simple, direct "I need to go to the nurse's office" or "I need to go to the rest room" should take care of it. Teachers generally understand without further question. If necessary, the girl should explain that her period has started and let the *teacher* be embarrassed! The girl certainly has nothing to be ashamed of.

A Closer Look at Being a Boy

Notice the differences between the boys illustrated on pages 39, 40, and 41. When it comes to puberty, every boy (just like every girl) is unique. At the time that is right for the individual, the pituitary gland signals the testicles to produce more of the male hormone **testosterone** (tess-TOSS-tuh-roan). The changes caused by the testosterone are often noticed at about eleven or twelve years old, but can come a year or more before or a year or more after this age. Some of these changes are as follows:

- The penis, testicles, and scrotum grow larger. Since genital size is a concern for many boys, the following information might help. In a grown man, the testicles are *usually* about 1 3/4 inches long. The penis is *usually* between 3 1/4 and 4 1/4 inches long when soft, and *usually* between five and seven inches long when **erect**. I emphasize *usually* because we are talking about what is *average*, not about what is *normal* or what *should* be.
- The penis and the scrotum darken in color.
- Hair begins to grow in the pubic area, in the underarms, and on the face, as well as on the body as a whole.
- The voice begins to deepen.
- Over fifty percent of all boys experience some swelling and tenderness of the breasts during puberty. The nipples may get a bit larger, the ring of colored flesh around the nipple may get wider and darker, and many boys notice a rather flat, button-like lump under one or both nipples. This is neither a sign of disease nor an indication that one is turning into a girl! It is one of the ways in which boys' bodies react to hormones. Once the amount of hormones becomes balanced, this condition passes.
- Boys tend to broaden at the shoulders during this phase of growth, and many begin to catch up in height with the girls.
- Boys begin to experience more frequent **erections** (ee-RECK-shunz). The penis is generally soft or limp. Sometimes, though, blood rushes into the penis, filling tiny hollow sacs inside the shaft. Muscles at the base of the penis tighten and keep the blood from flowing back into the body. This causes the penis to become larger, firmer, and to stand out from the body. This is an erection, and it can occur in males of all ages, starting even before birth.

An erection can be embarrassing when it happens at an inconvenient time.

Erections can result from touching the genitals, from the rubbing of tight clothing, from the need to urinate, from having thoughts about sex, or simply from being close to a person for whom one has special feelings. Boys and men experience erections several times while they are asleep and often awaken with an erection.

Sometimes erections happen with no obvious explanation. A boy might be thinking of just about anything and suddenly find himself with an erection. Part of the explanation has to do with the growing minds of growing girls and boys. Their minds are making connections between experiences and feelings. Do you know how a cool breeze causes goose bumps to appear on your arms? how sounds—a song you really enjoy listening to, an unexpected scream, or fingernails scratching across a chalkboard—can do the same thing? Sometimes goose bumps happen as we just *think* of these kinds of things.

As our bodies and minds grow, we react more strongly to what we see, hear, smell, taste, feel, and think. You used to look at a rock and see a rock. Now you might see that same rock, be reminded of someplace special you once visited, and even begin to have some of the same feelings you had during that visit. You don't have to work at those feelings. Your mind brings them back automatically. Such connections could be the reason behind the for-no-reason erections that boys experience more frequently during puberty.

Erections usually aren't noticed by anyone else and don't last forever. *Should* a boy find himself with an erection at a time when someone might notice it—whether that be in the locker room or in the middle of giving a report in front of the history class—he needs to remember that what he is experiencing is perfectly normal. He might try taking several deep breaths, focusing his attention on something other than the erection. Since there's nothing wrong with him or with what he's doing, there's no need to go to extremes to try to cover up or hide. As a boy moves out of adolescence and into adulthood, erections become less of a problem.

- Boys experience their first ejaculation. Ejaculation refers to what happens when the mixture of sperm and semen is pushed from the seminal vesicles into the urethra. As muscles automatically give a strong squeeze, the fluid is squirted from the penis. This ejaculation is accompanied by an orgasm which, as with girls, refers to very pleasant pulsing feelings in the genital area.

The first ejaculation happens for many boys somewhere around fourteen years of age, although it is perfectly normal for it to happen before or after this time. Some boys experience their first ejaculation during masturbation, which we'll discuss more in chapter 4. Other boys will have their first ejaculation while they are asleep. This is called a **nocturnal emission** (nock-TER-nal ee-MISH-uhn), or wet dream. It happens because the seminal vesicles are full of semen, and the mind is able during sleep to produce the kind of stimulation that leads to an orgasm. No need to worry! This is simply part of how God has designed the male body to relieve itself of sexual tension and excess semen. How often do wet dreams happen? That varies greatly from one boy to the next. Some boys *never* have them. It's OK if they do and OK if they don't.

We are created by God:

some of us female,
some of us male,
each of us special,
each of us sexual,
each of us growing at our own unique pace.

Many young people like you wonder and worry about whether their bodies are "on schedule" when it comes to physical development. The illustrations on the following three pages show five girls and five boys when they are around eleven, sixteen, and twenty-one years of age. As you look at these illustrations, note that bodies come in all different types at all ages.

Some young people begin to look quite mature in their mid-teens. For some this happens a few years earlier, and for others it happens a few years later. Remember that everyone is different. With all of the variety there is among bodies in God's world, you fit in quite nicely! What a fantastic creation *you* are!

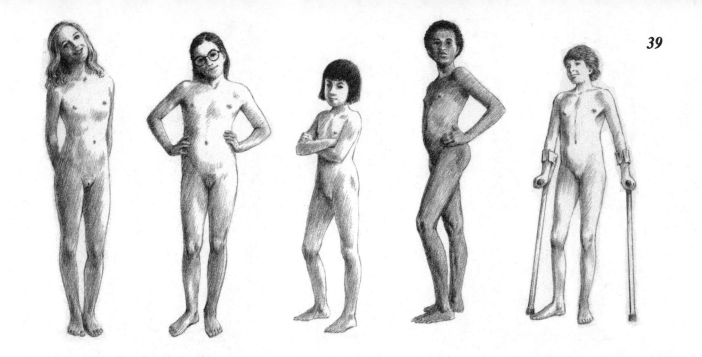

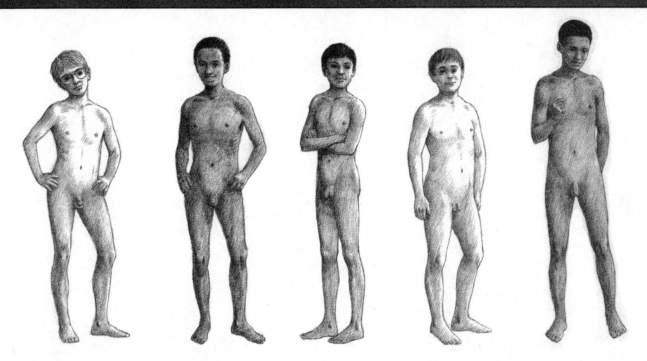

Around Eleven Years Old

40

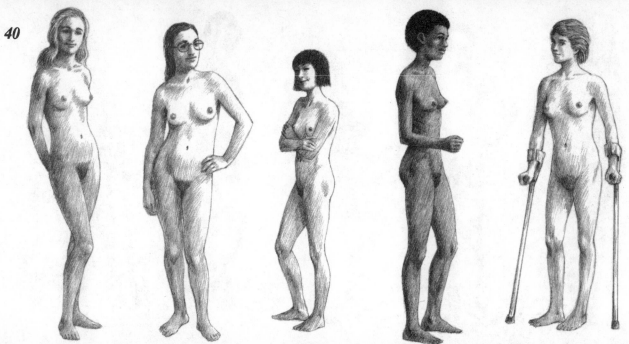

Around Sixteen Years Old

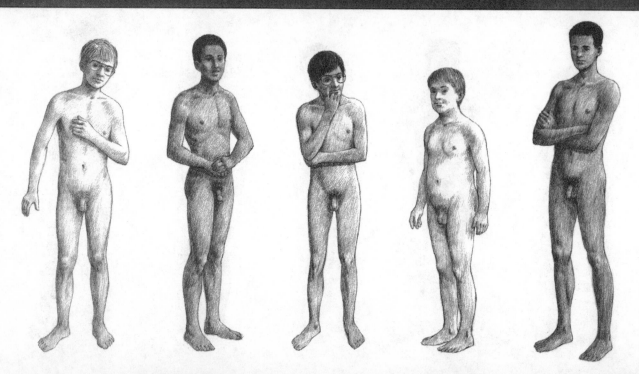

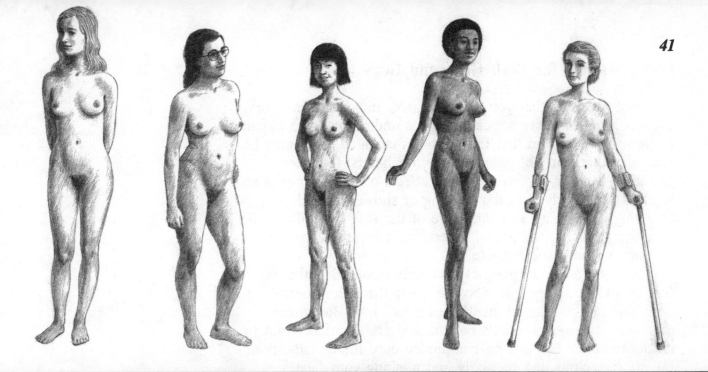

Around Twenty-one Years Old

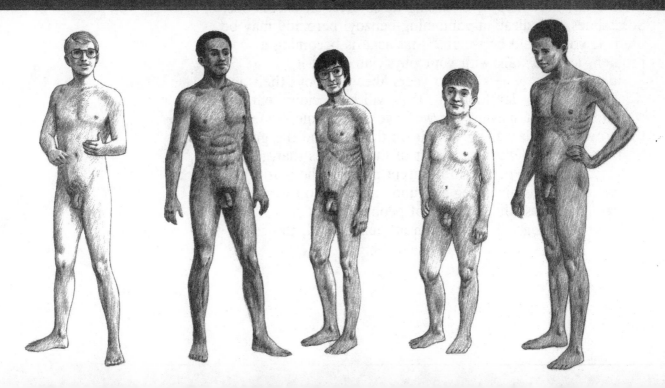

Some Matters for Both Girls and Boys

About the time that you begin to grow underarm hair, or even before, you may notice that your underarms have begun to perspire more and that the odor has changed. This may be true for other parts of your body—your hands, feet, and genitals—as well. Again, these are effects of the hormones at work in your body. Regular bathing or showering and changing of clothing may take care of the situation, although you may find that the use of a deodorant or antiperspirant makes you more comfortable.

Oily skin and acne (pimples) is another condition that is common to young people who are going through puberty. Yes, this can be blamed on the hormones too! But rather than just laying blame, let's be practical and consider what to do about acne. There is no guaranteed cure for the situation, but washing your hair regularly and washing your face, shoulders, back, and upper chest with a non-abrasive soap twice a day may help by cleansing those areas of excess oils. Sometimes a medication containing benzoyl peroxide may be used. If you should be worried that acne is becoming a problem for you, talk with your physician about it.

Since girls are generally two years ahead of boys their age when it comes to development, they will be deciding earlier what to do about shaving. As we have already mentioned, the growth and darkening of hair on the legs and the growth of hair in the underarms are part of the changes that go with puberty. Different people in different parts of the world have different opinions about leg and underarm hair on women. In the United States, the majority of people do not find underarm and leg hair on women attractive. Still, this is a decision that girls—some when they are your age—will have to make for themselves. Some girls find that their parents don't want them to start shaving too early. This is a subject that they will need to talk over with their parents.

All of these phenomena can be traced to the work of that special timing mechanism, the pituitary gland, and to the hormone signals it is sending through your body right this very minute. Pretty amazing stuff, wouldn't you say? It's all normal—and so, by the way, are you!

Oh what a wonderful, marvelous, glorious,
What a fantastic creation we are!
When I look all around I am reminded
We're far more amazing than earth, sea, and star![1]

WONDERFUL! MARVELOUS! GLORIOUS! FANTASTIC!

1 "What a Fantastic Creation We Are!" Copyright © 1984, 1987 by James Ritchie. Used by permission.

Chapter 3

Being Female, Being Male, Being You

The Difference Between Adam and Eve

The story of Adam and Eve is a story of people growing up. Long before it was written down, this tale was passed from one generation to the next by storytellers. Reading the story, I hear the storyteller chuckle a bit while explaining God's solution to Adam's need for companionship. *Animals!*

Adam was feeling lonely, so God provided him with pets—*lots* of pets! And God said to Adam, "Those are fine looking critters, Adam. What are you going to call them?" Giving names to all of the animals kept Adam busy for a while. However, it wasn't long before God realized that, nice as the animals were, they didn't meet Adam's need for a suitable companion.

God went to Plan B and created Eve to be Adam's suitable companion. Like Adam, she was human. But she was a *different* kind of human. Perhaps that's what made Eve so suitable! Adam and Eve could enjoy their sameness and at the same time enjoy exploring and discovering the many ways in which they were different. The Bible says that "The man and the woman were both naked, but they were not ashamed" (Genesis 2:25). Their differences were no problem to them. They were comfortable with themselves and comfortable with each other.

Unfortunately, Adam and Eve didn't *stay* comfortable. They made some poor decisions, and their relationship with God began to fall apart. They began looking for leaves to cover the most obvious of their differences—their bodies. As their relationship with God broke down, their differences became an embarrassment to them. They felt like performers pushed into the spotlight before being ready to go on!

In the Spotlight

It started without warning.

"Quit looking at me!" Pete shouted at his younger brother.

"I wasn't!"

"Mom, make him stop!"

"Stop what?" Mom asked as she came in the room to find out what the shouting was all about.

"Looking at me like that."

"Like what?" she asked.

"I don't know. He's just always *looking* at me."

While that conversation might not make much sense, it's one you recognize, isn't it? You probably understand exactly how Pete felt. Like many girls and boys your age, you sometimes feel as though you are on stage or standing in the spotlight. You sense that everyone is looking at you, watching what you are doing, grading your appearance, and rating your behavior. You feel that people are expecting you to look, to sound, to dress, and to *grow* a certain way. Even when people *aren't* watching, you *feel* as though they are. These are anxious feelings because there is no way that you or anyone else can meet all those expectations.

If young people had their way, everyone would look just about the same. No one would be the tallest or the shortest, the best or the worst dressed, the most or the least popular. Among the girls, no one would have the most or the least developed breasts. No one would be the first or the last to have her period or to begin shaving her legs and underarms. Among the boys, no one would have the greatest or the least amount of body hair or be the first or the last to have his voice change. Everyone would be the same. No one would stand out in the crowd.

Would that kind of sameness take some of the pressure off of you? Would it remove you from the stage or from the spotlight? Would sameness make everything *fair*?

It's Not Fair!

Fairness is a big concern for boys and girls your age. For my daughter, *fair* related to the kind of shoes she wore.

"I hate these shoes!" she said angrily. I could tell that we were in for an exciting shopping trip. "No one wears shoes like these! I can never find a pair of shoes I like!" Ever have the feeling that you know exactly what someone is going to say next? I did right then, and my daughter didn't prove me wrong. "It's not fair!" she stated loud enough for everyone in the store to hear.

"I know you're upset, and I understand," I said, trying to calm her down. "We've been through this before. You have a narrow foot. Those other shoes just won't fit. Is this pair all that bad?"

In her eyes, they *were* all that bad. Probably worse. And as far as she was concerned, I *didn't* understand. I thought to myself, *Why does shoe shopping always have to end like this?* Then I did some remembering. When I was in fifth and sixth grade, the big thing was penny loafers—slip-on shoes with a special place on top to tuck a penny in for decoration. No one *dared* to wear anything else! I remembered wanting to look just like my friends, and I understood my daughter's anger. She was right. It *wasn't* fair!

But *what* wasn't fair? My daughter couldn't wear the same kind of shoes that everyone else was wearing. Was that unfair? Maybe the unfairness was the "rule" that everyone had to wear the same kind of shoes to eliminate the differences between people.

Intimacy and Vulnerability: Two New Words

As the growth process causes differences among boys, among girls, and between girls and boys to become more and more obvious, it's easy for young people to begin moving farther and farther apart from each other. Comparing themselves to others, they decide who is better. That's called competition. Competition means that there are going to be winners and losers.

Maybe **intimacy** (IN-tuh-muh-see) isn't a new word to you. If you *have* heard it, you might have heard the word in connection with the sexual behavior that sometimes goes on between men and women. But intimacy is more than the closeness of bodies. Intimacy means a close friendship between *people*. Intimacy happens when people take the time to get to know each other's likes, dislikes, hopes, and fears; when they learn to accept each other just as they are. Intimacy is something that can happen between *any* two people who are willing to work at it.

Intimacy puts an end to competition. The object of intimacy is not to decide who is best, but to simply enjoy being together and getting to know one another. Think about the people with whom *you* feel most comfortable. Who are the people with whom you can just be yourself and not worry about who's watching you or who you need to look better than? Who are the people with whom you feel OK about admitting your mistakes and your weaknesses? These are the people with whom you are building intimacy.

Intimacy can be a scary thing because it exposes our **vulnerability** (vuhl-ner-uh-BILL-uh-tee). You know about Superman and kryptonite, don't you? Just like Superman, we all have our vulnerabilities—obstacles we can't overcome, things we either can't do or will never do well. There are some things we can never be. Boys can't be girls or know what it feels like to be a girl. Girls can't be boys or know what it feels like to be a boy. There are some things that we can only understand by getting close to other people. These are some of our vulnerabilities.

The key to intimacy is honesty. Being honest about our vulnerabilities can help make a relationship strong. Girls don't have to compete with one another to prove who is the best girl. Boys don't have to compete with one another to

prove who is the best boy. Girls and boys don't have to compete with each other to prove that either girls or boys are best. Intimacy is accepting and enjoying people for who they are. You don't have to be like everyone else. You don't have to be the best. Just be yourself!

I'll sing this song to celebrate myself;
I'll sing this song with pride;
Whatever I am is what God made,
And I have nothing to hide;
For God made me and God made you,
And God makes no mistakes!
So be yourself, and I'll be me;
That's all it really takes.[1]

Stereotypes

In listening to other people as they talk; reading books, magazines, and newspapers; watching movies; tuning in to television shows and commercials; singing along with song lyrics; and observing families and friends living, working, and playing together; we begin to form pictures in our minds. When the pictures get put together, they can suggest how people *ought* to be. Sometimes this kind of mental picture is called a **stereotype** (STAIR-ee-oh-type). Stereotypes are like shadows. Shadows are just outlines of what is really there. The shadow of one person is going to be pretty much like the shadow of another person. Everyone ends up looking pretty much the same.

A stereotype of males might suggest that all men are young, muscular, tall, and handsome. They wear the right clothes, have their hair styled the right way, say the right things, and fall in love with the right woman. A stereotype of females might try to convince us that all women are beautiful, young, and have well-shaped bodies. They always wear just the right shade of nail polish, lipstick, and eye makeup; are never seen in the same outfit twice in one month; and fall in love with the right man. These stereotypes do not describe all men or all women, but there are people spending millions of dollars every year to convince us that everyone ought to fit these stereotypes.

Celebrate Yourself!

Freedom is an idea that relates to all we have been talking about. Stereotypes confine people by telling them what they should or shouldn't be. Breaking stereotypes sets people free—free to be who they are and free to celebrate who they are. You may *want* to be like someone else, but you don't *have* to be like anyone else. You can feel great about being who you are!

Let's go a step further. Feeling good about yourself is something you have the *right* and the *responsibility* to do. A story from the life of Jesus might help us understand.

Jesus was once approached by a teacher of the Law who asked him, "Which commandment is the most important of all?" Jesus answered the question by quoting from the book of Deuteronomy. "Listen, Israel!" Jesus said. "The Lord our God is the only Lord. Love the Lord your God with all your heart, with all your soul, with all your mind, and with all your strength."

Jesus didn't stop there. He took what he considered to be the most important commandment and paired it with a second one: "Love your neighbor as you love yourself." Jesus said to the teacher of the Law, "There is no other commandment more important than these two" (adapted from Mark 12:28-31).

As you grow in your ability to understand what's going on around you, you are discovering that your feelings about God, about other people, and about yourself are all connected. If you aren't feeling good about yourself, it's pretty tough to put your whole self—heart, soul, mind, and strength—into loving God. If you haven't learned to love yourself, to say to yourself, *Hey! I'm OK just the way I am,* you're going to have a tough time loving your neighbor. Remember that *neighbor* can refer to anybody—not just the person who lives next door.

Building Bridges

When you feel good about yourself—including feeling good about your growing and changing body—you find lots of energy and enthusiasm to give to loving God and loving neighbor. You're all set to get at the task of building bridges—building intimacy—between people and between people and God. These good feelings about yourself have a lot to do with how you see yourself as a female or a male. They don't always happen automatically. They have to be worked at. I can't think of more important work for girls and boys like you to be doing.

Bridge building begins by learning about yourself. You learn to call the parts and functions of your body by their proper names. You learn to recognize some of the slang terms that are used to describe the same parts and functions. You don't have to *use* the slang terms, but you'll feel better if you know what they refer to. Have more information on hand than what you actually need.

Your expanded vocabulary will make it easier for you to talk to others about the thoughts and feelings you have about yourself. You'll also be able to better understand when others express *their* thoughts and feelings. You are building bridges with words, information, and understandings that you have in common with other persons.

It is important that girls build bridges with other girls. There are some things that only another girl can completely understand. Boys need to build bridges with other boys. Many people live with the stereotype that boys and men never share their feelings, that they can work out all of their problems on their own. Not so! Boys need to practice talking to each other about their feelings.

Girls and boys need to get to know each other by talking to each other. This particular kind of bridge building can prepare people for the possibility of being married some day. But whether or not they choose to be married, boys and girls need to build bridges between each other while they are young, simply because they live in a world where people come in two genders! The following stories may help you to see how important bridge building can be.

Friends: Paula and Tiffany

Paula and Tiffany had a problem! As their bodies began to change, they found that their nipples were becoming tender and were being irritated by the rubbing of their clothing. But their breasts hadn't developed much, and they were sure that their mothers wouldn't see the need for them to begin wearing bras.

They suffered separately for a while. Finally, Paula timidly mentioned the situation to Tiffany. Both were relieved to know that they weren't alone with the problem.

"I can't believe you've been going through the same thing!" Together they plotted. "If one of us can get her mother to agree to the bra, the other's mother is *sure* to go along with the idea!" They decided that at 5 o'clock they would both go to their mothers and tell them that they needed bras.

To their amazement, *both* mothers understood and agreed to take them shopping that evening for their first bras. Let's give those mothers some credit for remembering back to when they experienced the same thing. But let's also recognize two smart friends who managed to put their feelings into words and who tackled their problem *together*!

Friends: Carlos and Tim

They had been buddies since third grade, so Tim could tell something was wrong with his friend Carlos. Though he tended to be quiet, for the past three days Carlos had been almost *silent*. In hearing some boys talking after school, Tim finally figured out what was bothering Carlos.

Carlos and three other boys had had a backyard sleepout the weekend before. First they went through all of the ghost stories they knew. Then it was the dirty jokes. Not wanting the others to think that they didn't know all about sex, they laughed even when they didn't understand the jokes. One thing led to another, and they eventually ended up touching each other's genitals. Somehow the story got out, and after three days it was hard to say *who* had heard about it or *what* story they had heard.

Tim's first thought was that he would be better off to avoid Carlos. But he thought again. Whenever he found himself in a situation like this, Tim felt better if he could spend some time talking to God about it. That's what he did. The next afternoon he cornered Carlos.

"Want to talk?" asked Tim.

"About what?" Carlos replied.

"Friday night."

Carlos turned a bright red. "*You* heard?"

"Yeah."

Carlos started to run, but Tim grabbed his arm and stopped him. "Do you think you're the first one to do something like that?"

"I don't know. It was so *stupid*!" said Carlos.

"Maybe," Tim answered.

"Still want to be my friend?" asked Carlos.

"Still want to be *mine*?" asked Tim. Carlos looked puzzled as Tim blushed, took a deep breath, and continued. "I did practically the same thing." As Tim talked a little about his experience and feelings, Carlos began to relax. Tim was some special friend—the kind of friend who helps a person get through the tough parts of growing up.

Friends: Susan and Ronny

"Valerie Taylor likes you!" shouted Susan to Ronny as he headed toward home. Ronny turned, gave her a dirty look, and kept walking.

"Ronny, did you hear me? I said Val—"

"I *heard* you!" he interrupted. "The whole *neighborhood* heard you!"

"Sorry. Well, do you like her?"

"Like who?"

"Valerie Taylor! You said you *heard* me!"

"Me and everyone within five blocks of here."

"You still didn't answer me."

"I don't plan to."

"You make me so angry!" said Susan.

"You embarrass me," Ronny replied.

"I didn't think you *could* embarrass."

"Surprise!"

Susan thought for a moment. "I *am* sorry, Ronny. I guess I wasn't thinking."

I don't know where Valerie Taylor stands, but if Ronny and Susan can keep talking and listening and can be more sensitive to each other, they might even become friends!

Feminine and Masculine

You're beginning to have a better understanding of your body and of others' bodies as well. You're also working on your understanding of what it means to be **feminine** (FEHM-uh-nin) and **masculine** (MASS-kyuh-lin). So are Martin and Randy, two twelve-year-olds with heads full of stereotypes as to what twelve-year-old boys ought to look like. They're in the locker room at the YMCA.

As they stand under the showers, Martin is aware that his body hasn't started to develop yet. (By the way, Martin isn't the only one making such observations! It's just one of the things that growing boys and girls do.) Martin hasn't started to sprout any hair under his arms or around his genitals—quite normal for his age. Randy, on the other hand, is showing some of the signs of puberty, including the start of a moustache—also quite normal. Does one of these boys represent the stereotype for *all* boys their age?

Cindy and Dawn, two girls at a slumber party, have had their minds filled with stereotypes too. Cindy was ten years old when she had her first period. At twelve, she is one of the girls whose breasts are well developed. Dawn is three months older than Cindy but still hasn't had her first period and hasn't started wearing a bra yet. Do either Dawn or Cindy represent the stereotype for *all* twelve-year-old girls? Is one of these girls more *feminine* than the other?

People often affirm the appearance or the behavior of young girls by making comments such as, "Isn't she a little *lady*!" The same happens to young boys with comments like, "He's *all* boy!" People may mean well, but they aren't always helpful. Little girls are little girls—not ladies. It's not fair to expect a little girl to be a lady and miss being a little girl. Boys don't come half boy and half salamander. But people have a picture in their minds—a stereotype—of what girls and boys *should* be like. When they see things in girls and boys that match their mental pictures, they point these things out. What happens then? Boys and girls grow up thinking that all boys should be alike and that all girls should be alike. That's neither true nor fair.

When it comes to gender, you're either male or female; you're either a boy or a girl. There's nothing mysterious or uncertain about it. Gender is not something you have by degrees. You can't be more girl or less girl, or more boy or less boy than someone else. Chapter 4 will explain how gender or sex is determined. What you need to know now is that you are either male or female—*all* male or *all* female.

Feminine is something different. So is masculine. They have nothing to do with how early you develop, how late you develop, or how large or how small parts of your body are. *Femininity* is how a person chooses to express *her* understanding of what it means to be female. *Masculinity* is how a person chooses to express *his* understanding of what it means to be male. Different people express themselves in different ways. Some folks choose to express their femaleness or maleness in traditional ways. That's fine! Some choose not to be limited by what people have considered feminine and masculine in the past. That's fine too!

In Deborah's case, people questioned her decision to be a dentist like her father. *A receptionist in a dentist's office is a good job for a woman*, some thought. *If she wants to work on people's teeth, why doesn't she study to be a dental assistant?* No, Deborah wanted to be a dentist. Along with being a wife and a mother, that is what she's doing today.

Our son-in-law—the father of our twin grandchildren—fits all of the stereotypes related to being masculine. He's a tall, red-bearded fellow, with great big hands. But his height, his beard, and his hands don't express his understanding of what it means to be masculine. Part of being male for him is changing the diapers of the children he fathered, helping with the laundry, and getting up in the middle of the night for feedings. Being masculine is more than appearances. For our son-in-law, it's a matter of being a nurturing parent.

Possibilities—Open to All

Today girls and boys have similar dreams and share many of the same possibilites. Girls and boys both have an opportunity to receive an education. Both take part in athletics, babysit, bag groceries at the supermarket, mow the lawn, prepare meals, and wash the dishes. "That's a boy's job" or "Only girls do that" are comments made less often now than when your parents and your grandparents were your age.

Folks today don't make decisions based only on how things have *always* been. When they *do* give thought to what people believed or how people behaved in the past, they will often ask, *But is that right?* Both men and women are employed outside the home today. Women go to the office, travel on business, and support their families financially. Not so long ago, these were considered men's tasks. Men spend much more time these days caring for children, doing the marketing, cooking, and cleaning. A few years ago these were things that, in most families, only women did.

Many of the stereotypes are gone. Boys and girls are becoming aware that, first of all, they are persons. The decisions they make about who they are and about what they will become are being made long before the matter of their gender is ever considered. Questions such as *What kind of work is right for a man?* and *What kind of work is right for a woman?* are being replaced by *What do I enjoy doing? What am I good at? What kinds of work would I rather avoid? What things frighten me? What sacrifices am I willing to make in order to reach my goals?* and *What needs are there in the world and how might God be able to use me in meeting those needs?*

---

1 "Song to Celebrate Myself" by Jerry O. Cook. Copyright © 1973 by Graded Press. Reprinted by permission of Jerry O. Cook.

Chapter 4

What to Do With This Wonderful Gift

You don't remember it, of course, but several years ago the special union of two persons resulted in something new—YOU! "Congratulations! It's a girl!" or "It's a boy!" were words that started you on the road to who you are now. Your gender—being female or male—was a gift to you. The mystery of that gift is something you can spend a lifetime wondering about, exploring, and enjoying.

As you grow and develop, you might think, "Now that I'm nearing or going through puberty, I'm becoming a *sexual* being!" The truth is that you've always been a sexual being. God didn't create us male, female, and put-this-one-on-hold-until-it-turns-twelve-and-then-we'll-decide. You were a male or a female from the moment of your **conception** (kuhn-SEP-shun). Your body began responding in sexual ways even before you were born. Doctors tell us that even in the womb, males experience erections and females experience vaginal lubrication. These responses are sexual. Boys respond as they do because they are males; girls respond as they do because they are females. Such responses do not necessarily mean that a person is *thinking* about sex or *feeling* sexy.

So Much to Learn

From the time you were born, you learned by experiencing the world around you. You looked, listened, smelled, tasted, and touched. You have been curious about your body since you were a baby. Back then people delighted in your reactions to the discovery of your hands and feet. You eventually learned to point to and name your ears, nose, eyes, mouth, and other body parts. You investigated what each one did.

One morning our telephone rang. When I answered I heard the familiar voice of our daughter's kindergarten teacher. "She has put a bean up her nose, and we can't get it out!"

I drove to the school, collected one daughter complete with one bean stuck up her nose, and headed for the doctor.

After the bean was removed and we were on our way home, I asked her, "Why did you put the bean in your nose?"

"I wanted to see what would happen." Sure enough, she had!

Do you recall or have your family members told about similar experiments that *you* performed? Like our daughter, curiosity has led you to some important discoveries about yourself. Exploring the *feel* of your body, you became aware of and discovered its various parts—including your genitals. Later, your curiosity might have drawn you into playing house or playing doctor with other children. Children want to see and touch the similarities and differences between themselves and their playmates—both male and female.

Masturbation

As a result of such exploration, children discover that touching the genitals causes pleasant sensations. Boys learn that rubbing the penis will cause an erection and, as they get older, an ejaculation. Girls have the same feelings when they touch or rub the vulva and the clitoris.

Girls and boys also find that this activity sometimes evokes rather strong responses from adults. Some adults attempt to halt the activity with a firm, "Stop that!" Others hurriedly try to distract the child. In such cases, children quickly learn that these activities do not meet with adults' approval. The confusion that results is understandable! *Why is it,* children might wonder, *that such nice feelings come from actions that are considered wrong?* This might be a question you're asking yourself right now.

The Bible's silence on the topic of masturbation suggests that it is not a moral problem. The troublesome thing about masturbation is the worry it causes. People worry that they will be caught, worry that others will somehow know that they have been masturbating, worry that they might harm themselves. While rough handling of the genitals could cause temporary irritation and soreness, masturbation is unlikely to damage the sexual organs. Males will not "run out" of semen or sperm if they masturbate. Their bodies will continue to produce more. Masturbation does not affect one's ability to enjoy sexual relations as an adult.

As you think about all of the opportunities, challenges, and fun that is available in the world God has created for us, you may conclude along with me that doing things that cause us to worry a lot doesn't make much sense. For many people, masturbation fits into this category. *Most* people masturbate at some time during their lives, and *many* continue to do so *throughout* their lives. In spite of its being a very natural experience, some worry about masturbation. If it should become a worrisome thing for you, remember that the problem is *worry*, not *masturbation*.

Still, anything we do that takes up too much of our time and energy, or keeps us apart from other people, needs to be questioned. What is too much? That's hard to say. Researchers have talked with many people about masturbation. These researchers have found that more males masturbate and masturbate more often than females. Some people masturbate several times a day; some, every day or so; some, just once in a while; and some never masturbate at all. There is no way to say what is right or normal. You will have to decide this for yourself.

You want to be doing things that make you feel good about yourself. Feeling good about yourself, as we talked about in chapter 3, helps you to love others and to love God. If masturbation seems to prevent you from feeling good about yourself, build a bridge! Find someone to talk with—a friend, a parent, or another adult you trust. Sometimes just talking with an understanding person helps relieve the worry.

Friends of the Same Gender

The years of childhood and adolescence are some of the most exciting. With so much change happening, it's hard to know what to expect next. Put *two* changing people together and you more than *double* the excitement! Because of all the change, friendships are not always easy during these years, but they are important, and they are often very strong. Right now your best friends are probably girls if you are a girl, and boys if you are a boy. Girls and boys are sometimes concerned about these friendships because they hear about **homosexual** persons—people who are sexually attracted to or sexually active with people of their own sex.

"Does this mean I'm homosexual?" a boy asked me after having thought about his closest friends—all of whom were boys.

"No, it doesn't," I assured him. "Children and preteens enjoy being with those who share their interests. These interests may be sports or drama or music or—well, you name it. What happens is that girls generally find themselves spending most of their time with other girls, and boys with other boys. Sharing interests and activities has nothing to do with homosexuality."

It is not unusual for sexual contact between boys and between girls to take place after the playing house or playing doctor that goes on between children. Again, this is, for some young people, a way of investigating the new bodies and new feelings that have come with adolescence. Having special feelings for a same-sex friend is very typical of people your age. This behavior and these feelings are *not* to be confused with homosexuality.

Something else that is very common at your age is the boy who has very strong feelings for a man—a teacher, coach, or camp counselor, for example. Girls your age often have strong feelings for women in similar positions. Having these feelings does not mean that they are homosexuals. Young people are thinking about who they are becoming. They see qualities in others that they like—qualities they hope that others will someday see in them.

These qualities might be related to personality; they might be physical qualities. It is natural to be attracted to people we admire. You have not invented something new! Make a list of all the things you admire in such a person. You might want this list to become part of the goals that you set for yourself. This is also an excellent subject for prayer. It is good for you to talk with God about the person you are becoming. You might also want to ask God to help you find just the right person with whom you can share these thoughts and feelings.

Boy-Girl Friendships

Although for some it comes earlier and for some later, it is usually during the teen years that boys and girls begin to be interested in persons of the other sex. They find that they *like* being together—quite a change from just a few years before when boys and girls wanted nothing to do with each other! They begin to date and to enjoy the closeness of holding hands, dancing, hugging, and kissing. They tell each other about their hopes, their dreams, and their concerns.

They are discovering that people who are very different from them *can* understand their personal thoughts and feelings. While they have been learning about commitment and loyalty through same-sex friendships, they now see commitment and loyalty from a new perspective—from the perspective of the other sex. They learn to communicate in new ways—through smiles, gentle touches, and being close. These are experiences that prepare young people for lasting relationships.

Adults, as well as older brothers and sisters who think that they know everything, sometimes joke about these first boy-girl relationships, referring to them as puppy love. But such friendships are often intense, consuming, and emotional experiences—in part because adolescents tend to experience *everything* in intense, consuming, and emotional ways. Joking about these friendships isn't helpful because they are valuable experiences. They help young people grow emotionally and practice responsible decision making. These early relationships are important ways in which new emotions are discovered and tested out. Such experiences will help you get to know the special adult person you are in the process of becoming.

A New Family

In time, most people find someone with whom they want to share their lives. They dream and make plans for a life together. They talk about the sharing of experiences and possessions and, in many cases, plan for the shared experience of parenting.

What can I do to make the one I love happy? is an important concern of husbands and wives. They soon learn that being faithful, honest, and open are some of the keys. They discover the joy of giving and receiving, the joy of exploring all the interesting things about another person. They respect the ways in which each is different and allow each other the freedom to follow individual interests, but they remain committed to the relationship. They laugh together and cry together. They talk to each other about what they are feeling and what they believe. The love they feel at first grows stronger as they meet the challenges of their life together.

Living Together as Husband and Wife

That is why a man leaves his father and mother and is united with his wife, and they become one.

Genesis 2:24

When two people love each other and share their lives in marriage, they express their love in many ways. A part of most marriages is the joy of sharing bodies in sexual intercourse. I say *most* because there are situations—during illness or as a result of physical limitations—when couples are unable to have sexual intercourse. Such couples discover other ways, through touch and being close, to express tender feelings for each other.

Sexual intercourse is one way in which husbands and wives celebrate the friendship and commitment they share. Their thoughts, words, touches, and kisses prepare them for sexual intercourse. Such actions are referred to as **foreplay** (FOR-play). In response, the man's penis becomes erect. The woman's outer genitals swell and her vagina becomes moist or lubricated, allowing the man to insert his penis easily inside the vagina. As their bodies move together, the pleasant feelings become increasingly stronger. At the peak of the man's sexual excitement, he experiences an orgasm, during which he ejaculates. The woman can also experience an orgasm—the intense and pleasant pulsing of the vaginal walls and of the entire genital area. Some people describe these feelings as being like a wave washing over. Orgasm is the point at which the waves of feelings break over them. Following orgasm, the couple relaxes and both enjoy a sense of contentment.

The frequency of sexual intercourse varies greatly between couples. Couples must decide what feels right for them. Most married adults, including your parents, express their love for each other in this way. The physical expression of love in marriage is celebrated in the Bible in verses such as ". . . be happy with your wife and . . . let her charms keep you happy; let her surround you with her love" (Proverbs 5:18-19) and "My lover is mine, and I am his" (Song of Songs 2:16a).

Where Babies Come From

Having a baby can be a very special time—both for the parents-to-be and for others who love them. In chapter 2 we described how once every month or so, an ovum is released from one of a female's ovaries into the fallopian tube. If that ovum joins with a sperm from the male, **conception** takes place, and new life has begun.

You created every part of me;
   you put me together in my mother's womb.
I praise you because you are to be feared;
   all you do is strange and wonderful.
   I know it with all my heart.
When my bones were being formed,
   carefully put together in my mother's womb,
when I was growing there in secret,
   you knew that I was there—
   you saw me before I was born.

Psalm 139:13-16a

Each time a male ejaculates, millions of tiny life-giving sperm are released with the semen. Each sperm is equipped with a tail to propel it from the vagina, through the uterus, and into the fallopian tube. The first sperm to reach the ovum and penetrate the outer shell is responsible for **fertilization** (fer-tuhl-uh-ZAY-shun). At that instant, many things are determined.

In chapter 2 we mentioned the genes that determine which traits you will inherit from your parents—hair, skin, and eye color; height; when and how quickly you will mature; and so forth. The genes are located on the **chromosomes** (KROH-muh-sohms) which are part of every cell in your body. One of the chromosomes that is contributed by the ovum is an X chromosome. The sperm can contain either an X or a Y chromosome. If the ovum is fertilized by a sperm with an X chromosome, the resulting XX combination will produce a girl. If the ovum is fertilized by a Y-carrying sperm, the XY combination will produce a boy.

While we're talking about the sex of an unborn baby, I have a story that might interest you. During her pregnancy, our daughter's doctor ordered an ultrasound examination. The technician ran an instrument over our daughter's abdomen that listened for the heartbeats and then noted the development of the twins on the monitor. "Do you want to know their sexes?" asked the technician.

"You bet!" our son-in-law responded.

"Well," said the technician, "Baby A is clearly a boy. See, there's the penis. And I think Baby B is a girl. There's no sign of a penis." That was at 26 weeks into the pregnancy. Sure enough, several weeks later we were holding a boy named William and a girl named Sarah. However, this particular method is not always accurate. Another method by which the sex can be determined is called **amniocentesis** (AM-nee-oh-sen-TEE-sis). A needle is inserted through the mother's abdomen and into the **amniotic** (am-nee-AH-tik) **sac** that surrounds the baby. A sample of the fluid from the sac is withdrawn. The analysis of this fluid sample is intended to detect possible birth defects, but will also indicate the gender of the baby.

From Embryo to Fetus

Let's get back to the fertilized ovum. The fertilized ovum divides again and again, as it moves from the fallopian tube into the uterus. In the uterus it attaches to the carpet-like lining. This cluster of fast-growing cells is called an **embryo** (EM-bree-oh). After three months, the embryo is called a **fetus** (FEE-tuhs).

The specific connection between the embryo and the mother is the **umbilical** (uhm-BILL-uh-kuhl) **cord** that links the embryo to the placenta. Food and oxygen are received directly from the mother's bloodstream through the umbilical cord. The elimination of waste takes place in the same way. Because of this direct linkage, an expectant mother is advised to eat properly, to avoid all drugs unless they are prescribed by her doctor, and to avoid alcohol and cigarettes. Whatever the mother takes into her body, she shares with her growing child. The abuse of one's body during pregnancy can seriously affect the child's development.

A Time to Be Born

The length of an average pregnancy is nine months or 40 weeks. At the end of that time the pituitary gland secretes a hormone that causes the birthing process to begin. The muscles of the uterus begin to shorten or contract. These **contractions** (kuhn-TRACK-shuns) are mild and far apart in the beginning of **labor**. As labor continues, they are stronger, come more often, and last longer. The contractions push the baby downward toward the **cervix** (SIR-viks)—the opening at the lower end of the uterus. The increasing pressure of the baby against the cervix causes the cervix to **dilate** (DIE-late) or open up.

At some point during labor, the amniotic sac breaks and the woman feels a gush or leaking of fluid as it flows from the uterus and out of the vagina. If you have heard people talk about an expectant mother whose water broke, this is what they were talking about. If the sac has not broken on its own during labor, the doctor will break it. Once the cervix has opened enough for the baby to pass through, the baby, usually head first, is pushed through the vagina and out of the body—the step called **delivery**.

Giving birth is hard work for the mother, which explains why the time it takes to position a baby for birth is called labor. It is a time of considerable discomfort. Many couples spend the last several weeks of pregnancy attending childbirth training classes. In these classes the couple is instructed in proper breathing techniques, how to focus attention on something other than the pain, and how the father can coach the mother during labor and delivery. Simply *knowing* about labor and delivery can help reduce worries and reduce discomfort. Also, there are a variety of medications that can be given to the mother, if needed, to relieve the pain in the latter part of labor and delivery.

Once the baby is born, the umbilical cord is cut, separating him or her from the mother. The contractions continue until they push the placenta out of the uterus. For several weeks following the delivery, bleeding may continue as the mother's body rids itself of tissue that was required during pregnancy but is no longer needed.

Caesarean Section Deliveries

Although most births are vaginal deliveries (babies delivered through the vagina) in the method just described, others are delivered by **caesarean** (sih-ZARE-ee-uhn) **section**.

The doctor makes an incision through the abdominal wall of the mother and lifts the baby from the uterus. Such deliveries are normal, and babies born by caesarian section are as healthy as those delivered vaginally. Mothers giving birth by caesarian section may need a longer time to recover than do mothers who deliver vaginally.

A caesarian section may be performed when the baby is in a **breach** position (not head first) that would make vaginal delivery dangerous for the baby or the mother. Occasionally a mother has a medical problem that makes vaginal delivery impossible or unsafe. Multiple births frequently require surgical delivery. My twin grandchildren were delivered by caesarean section. William, who would have been born first, was breach. The doctors determined that it would take too long to deliver him vaginally. The delay could have endangered his life and that of Sarah, who was also waiting to be born.

Multiple Births

As you can imagine, being the grandmother of twins gives me an interest in multiple births. I also know that boys and girls are often curious as to how it happens that a mother will give birth to more than one baby. Do you recall that following conception, the cells begin to divide? Sometimes these cells split completely apart, and two babies develop instead of one. These babies are always of the same sex and are considered **identical** because they developed from the same ovum and sperm.

Sometimes the ovary releases more than one ovum. These ova are then fertilized by different sperm, and two or more embryos develop. These multiple babies are called **fraternal** and since they were fertilized by different sperm, they may or may not be the same sex.

What Else Might Be on Your Mind?

The subject of pregnancy always raises all kinds of questions. Perhaps we can answer a few of them.

"How does a woman know when she is pregnant?"

Once pregnancy has occurred, the menstrual periods stop, so not having a period is the first sign that a woman is pregnant. However, since other factors—involvement in athletics, poor health, and emotional stress, for example—can affect the regularity of the menstrual cycle, other special tests must be done to make sure that a woman is pregnant.

Some women experience what is often called **morning sickness**. Particularly during the first three months, women may have an upset stomach in response to their pregnancy. Many who experience this condition do so in the morning, although this is not always the case. Other changes in the body are signs of pregnancy. The breasts become sensitive to the touch and enlarge, preparing to produce milk for the mother to breastfeed her baby if she chooses to feed her baby in this way. The abdomen enlarges to accommodate the baby growing inside. As the uterus grows, it presses on the bladder, causing a pregnant women to need to urinate more often.

"Do couples have sexual intercourse during pregnancy?"

Yes. The fetus is well-protected in the uterus. The amniotic sac is filled with fluid that serves to cushion the baby inside. Unless there is a problem with the pregnancy where the mother must be unusually careful, most couples may continue having sexual intercourse until close to the time of birth.

"I guess I knew that my parents had sexual intercourse. After all, they had me! But I never thought that they did it regularly!"

Few parents talk freely with their children about this part of their marriage. Sexual intercourse is a private thing that husbands and wives enjoy together. At the same time, children need to know that this *is* a part of their parents' relationship. Sometimes girls and boys interpret their parents' silence as evidence that their mothers and fathers are *not* sexually active. So when they begin to have sexual feelings about someone and need to make some important decisions, they assume that their parents won't understand.

Many children (maybe *you*) have had the experience of rushing in unannounced to their parents' bedroom and finding Mom and Dad in a moment of sexual closeness. Beyond the embarrassment, there is something to be learned. Parents *do* enjoy the physical part of being in love, and they need private times to express their love in a way that God fully intended for them. Yes, your parents will understand your sexual feelings. They *have* had and *continue* to have those feelings too.

"Why should I wait until I'm married to have sexual intercourse?"

It's true that from early adolescence young people are physically capable of sexual intercourse. Girls and boys become sexually excited. Unfortunately, some allow themselves to get into situations where sexual intercourse can and does happen.

Remember the word *intimacy* that we talked about in chapter 3? As we said back then, intimacy is much more than a closeness of bodies. Intimacy is a closeness of whole persons. Intimacy is two persons really knowing each other. Intimacy is loving another person just as he or she is.

For many people, sexual intercourse becomes a *part* of intimacy. But sexual intercourse and intimacy are *not* the same thing. Intimacy takes time. It grows best as two people *talk* with each other—talk about what makes them laugh, what makes them cry, what makes them angry, what makes them want to do their best, what makes them want to give up. Intimacy requires honesty, and honesty is pretty difficult for two young people who have allowed themselves to become involved in sexual intercourse.

Why wait to have sexual intercourse? Because young people who have sexual intercourse end up missing out on all of the talking that leads to intimacy. They're generally feeling guilty and embarrassed about what has happened and can't bring themselves to talk with each other about sex or about anything else. Sexual intercourse is a good gift, but when this good gift is used unwisely, it can *destroy* intimacy. The key is this: *intimacy first*.

In writing to the people of the Corinthian church, Paul provides an excellent working definition of love. Two of the qualities that Paul lists to describe love are *patience* and *kindness*. Paul also lists several things that love is *not*. One of these is *selfish*. Selfishness does not grow love; selfishness does not create intimacy.

Waiting—being patient—is seldom easy, but you'll be doing quite a bit of it in the next few years. Being patient when it comes to sexual intercourse is an act of kindness—toward yourself, toward that person for whom you have special feelings, and toward the many other people who stand to be affected if you make the decision to have sexual relations while you are young. Setting yourself up to feel guilty is foolish. Not thinking of the many people who will be affected by your actions is unkind and selfish. Young people are fooling themselves when they think that their sexual relations are their own business.

Perhaps you've read or heard how important it is for babies to crawl before they walk. Something is happening during the crawling stage that helps develop the coordination between a little person's eyes and hands. Important stuff is happening during that period when one is waiting to walk. Children who walk before they crawl or who spend too little time crawling may have coordination-related difficulties later on.

So it is with sexual intercourse. Young people are wise to wait. Those who choose *not* to wait run the risk of never discovering the special blessings that God offers through our sexual union with another person. Creating intimacy requires that we spend time together doing the things that help us get to know each other. In doing so, we build the foundation for wonderful friendships and, perhaps, for the enjoyment of sexual relations with one to whom we have made a life-long commitment.

"What is a virgin?"

In biblical times the word **virgin** meant a young woman but was also used to refer to a woman who had not yet had sexual intercourse. The same word now applies to both females and males.

An unstretched or untorn hymen was once believed to be the proof that a girl was still a virgin. Tradition said that a true virgin would bleed when the hymen was penetrated by the penis during the first experience of sexual intercourse. As was mentioned in chapter 2, there are many factors that can account for the absence of the hymen. The presence or absence of the hymen is not proof of a female's virginity.

"Does it hurt to have sexual intercourse?"

Generally, no. I say "generally" because that answer needs a couple of explanations. The first is this: since the vagina of a female who has not had sexual intercourse has not been stretched, she may experience some discomfort the first time or two that she has intercourse. The second is connected to the differences between how men and women respond to sexual stimulation.

Men respond more quickly and thus tend to be ready for sexual intercourse before their partners are ready. Women respond more gradually and are stimulated by loving words and touches. If intercourse is attempted before a woman is ready physically and emotionally, it can be uncomfortable for both persons. "Love is patient," said Paul, and so it is (I Corinthians 13:4). A loving man will be sensitive to his partner's needs and not try to rush into something for which his partner is not ready.

"When are people finished being sexual?"
Never. Being sexual is part of what it means to be human. Since we are human at the moment of our conception and continue to be human throughout life, we are *sexual* all of that time as well.

Our society is paying more attention and being more sensitive to the sexuality of people who we once treated as non-sexual. You, for instance. Girls and boys are sexual beings with sexual thoughts and sexual feelings. Another example is older adults who continue to need intimacy and physical closeness long after they have ceased to fit the stereotypes for sexy women or men.

People who are ill and people who have physically or mentally handicapping conditions are human and are sexual. Their sexual needs are human needs. To be created in the image of God is to be created male or female. We are slowly learning to respect and to understand the sexual part of all God's human creatures.

What About the Rest of My Questions?

As a young child you asked many questions about many different subjects. Growing older, you probably became aware that some adults are uncomfortable with questions about bodies and sexuality. Some put off giving answers, saying, "Let's discuss this later." Some pretend not to hear the questions.

So young people may decide to stop asking such questions. Making adults uncomfortable seldom pays off. But the questions remain. There is much that you need to know about your body and about your sexuality. Where do you go for answers? I trust that you're finding some of those answers as you read this book, but I also realize that there is no way that one book is going to answer every question being asked by girls and boys your age. Let's explore some sources for the answers that you need.

Begin with family members. Your parents, grandparents, aunts, uncles, older sisters, brothers, and cousins have had the same questions and concerns that you are having now. Really! They might need to be reminded that they were once your age, since people sometimes forget.

Many things have changed since your parents and grandparents were experiencing adolescence. That's important for *you* and for *them* to remember. If you have brothers or sisters who are considerably older than you, some things will have changed since the time *they* were your age. The music you listen to, the television shows and movies that you watch, and the books that you read are just a few examples of changes that have taken place.

Some values and rules have changed as well. My grandfather shook his head in disbelief when he discovered my brother, sister, and me playing cards—*on Sunday*! That would never have happened in his home, but in our's it was accepted.

I smile as I observe the children and teenagers in our church. When I was their age, everyone got dressed up for Sunday school and worship. Now I see many of my young friends wearing jeans and tennis shoes when they are at the church. Things change. One way may not be better than others. They're just different.

But some values haven't changed. Love and commitment between two persons who plan to share their lives will always be crucial. Families are important. Our families are the primary place for our discovery of values—those attitudes, qualities, and beliefs that are important to us and that help us as we make our decisions. In our families we learn the rules that help protect us—not just limit our freedom to do the things we want.

The young person who talks with and listens to family members will find answers to many questions. If they are uncomfortable with your questions, don't give up! Give them another chance at it—and another, and another if that's what it takes. It *will* pay off!

Look to other responsible adults such as your teachers, pastors, Sunday school teachers, friends' parents, coaches, pediatrician or family doctor, school counselors, and scout leaders. Maybe they'll have answers to your questions, and maybe they won't. If they don't, they'll probably be willing to give you a hand at finding the information you need. There are times when it's easier to talk with someone who is *not* a parent—or at least not *your* parent. We are afraid that we will worry or upset our parents by asking some questions. But we still need answers. Go get them!

Talk with your friends. Are friends good sources of information? Sometimes they are and sometimes they aren't. There is something that they *are* good sources of: *friendship*! Friends often understand how you're feeling because they are feeling or have felt the same way. They could be confused about the same things that *you're* confused about. So, talk! Don't wait until you're all grown up to say to a friend, "When we were in sixth grade, I was worried sick about going into seventh. I felt like I was growing up so slowly and was sure that I was going to stick out like a sore thumb among all those *big* junior high kids;" and have that friend respond, "I thought that *I* was the only one who felt like that! Why didn't we tell each other about those feelings?"

Books can be good sources of accurate information. When you have questions about what's going on inside and outside your body—read, read, read! Study the diagrams and read what the writer has to say. If your church has a library, you might find some helpful books there. The public library is another good source of information. In the back of this book you'll find a list of other readings that could be helpful to you. As you read, you'll probably come up with new questions to ask.

Your sexuality *is* a wonderful gift! You'll have many decisions to make in the years ahead as to what you'll do with this wonderful gift. The many questions you have now and will have in the future will help you to make those decisions. *Ask* those questions, and *keep asking* until you get the answers you need!

Chapter 5

What's Out There? Becoming Aware

Becoming an adolescent means having more opportunities to be on your own and to be making your own decisions. In this chapter we'll talk frankly about things that can affect your well being. The questions are ones that boys and girls raise during human sexuality studies taking place in churches all over the country—questions that *I* have been asked many times.

Is this chapter going to be all gloom and doom? No, it's not. I agree with Paul when he suggests to the Philippians that they fill their minds with "those things that are good and that deserve praise: things that are true, noble, right, pure, lovely, and honorable" (from Philippians 4:8). In order to make room for all of these good things, we need to clear out negatives such as ignorance and worry.

Dating

What's it like to go out on a date? How old do I have to be? What should I do? What *shouldn't* I do?

Dating is not something that *many* people your age are doing, although *some* are. In any case, it's natural for you to be wondering what happens on a date.

Dating is one way young people get to know each other. In many ways, dating is like any other act of friendship. You talk, laugh, do things, and go places together. Friendships generally start with things that people have in common: Living near each other, liking the same kind of music, playing on the same team, sitting beside each other in class—those sorts of things. Friends who are *dating* have things in common too, but the fact that they are not of the

same sex adds a new and special element. People are drawn together not just because they are *alike* in many ways, but because they are *different*.

First-time daters are usually nervous. They have to think through some new questions: How do I order if we go out to eat? Do we pay for our own meals or movie tickets or does the boy always pay for both? Should we be holding hands? What about kissing—who starts and when is it okay? What time should we be in?

Remember the intimacy issue? Here it comes again! Dating can be fun—especially when people *talk* to each other. Be *honest*. Tell your date how nervous you feel. Chances are, your date feels the same way. Decide ahead of time who's going to pay for the meal or the movie. Why not share the expenses?

Dating can present problems when respect for self and others isn't given a high priority. Be smart. Understand yourself, your feelings, and the way your mind and body react when you are close to another person, holding hands, hugging, and kissing. *Talking* together about these matters shows your care and respect for each other.

Being in Love

How will I know when I'm in love?

This is a great question, and one that many people your age are probably wondering about. You see people in love. You see people who once were in love but aren't any more. Were they *really* in love, or did they make a mistake? The lives of many girls and boys have been touched directly by the divorce of parents or indirectly by the divorce of other family members, neighbors, or friends' parents. Are there ways to avoid making mistakes?

We start by realizing that we were created by God to love *many* people, not just *one*. There are many people who are *possible* life-long partners for us, not just one. You will be meeting lots of people in the next several years. You will be developing friendships with some of those people. With some of those friends you will work at building intimacy. Perhaps there will be one special person you will decide to marry—one person to whom you will commit your life.

The question *How will I know when I'm in love?* tends to be more a question of *feeling* than of *knowing*. We expect that our bodies are going to give us some very specific signals. It's true that our bodies *do* respond in certain ways when we are attracted to another person. But the responses of our bodies don't always tell us who we should or shouldn't consider as marriage partners.

Let me give you some other questions to ask yourself. Who do I enjoy being with more than anyone else? Who makes me feel good about myself? Who do I always enjoy discovering new things about? Who values the things I consider to be important? Who wants to be *close* to me but doesn't insist that we do *everything* together? Who do I trust with my personal thoughts and feelings?

In some marriage services, the pastor concludes the ceremony with these words to the couple:

God the Eternal keep you in love with each other,
  so that the peace of Christ may abide in your home.
Go to serve God and your neighbor in all that you do.

Then the pastor says to everyone,

Bear witness to the love of God in this world,
  so that those to whom love is a stranger
  will find in you generous friends.[1]

What you feel *for* and experience *with* one person sometimes helps you to feel complete and to be more loving toward others. This may be a good sign that you are in love.

---

1 From *A Service of Christian Marriage.* © 1979 by The United Methodist Publishing House. Reprinted by permission.

Homosexuality

I think that I understand *what* a homosexual is, but *why* are some people homosexuals?

A person who is **heterosexual** (het-uh-roh-SEK-shoo-uhl) is sexually attracted to or sexually active with persons of the other sex. A person who is homosexual is sexually attracted to or sexually active with persons of the same sex. Both male and female homosexuals are sometimes referred to as being **gay**, although this word is mostly used in reference to male homosexuals. Female homosexuals are sometimes referred to as **lesbians** (LEZ-bee-uhnz). *Gay* and *lesbian* are words many homosexual persons use to speak of their sexuality. A **bisexual** person is one who is sexually attracted to or sexually active with persons of both sexes. While these three sexual orientations may appear to be very distinct or separate, in reality the divisions are not so clear. Every individual is different.

Why are some people homosexuals? Much research has been done on the subject by doctors, psychologists, educators, and theologians; but they have yet to agree on a reason. So the honest answer to the question is this: *We do not know*.

Can you tell just by looking that a person is a homosexual? No, you can't. Though a female does not fit the stereotype for femininity—that is, if she tends to be a kind of rough-and-tumble type—we must not assume that this says something about her sexual orientation. Likewise, if a male tends to be more interested in arts than in sports, we cannot assume anything about his sexual orientation. Observing a person's interests, behaviors, or body type cannot tell us what that person's sexual orientation might be.

Not having clear-cut answers, we tend to feel confused and even afraid—feelings that sometimes cause us to be less than loving. Learning about things—and people—that frighten and confuse us can take away the fear and confusion.

Instead of basing our actions on what we *don't* know—such as why people represent a variety of sexual orientations—we need to act on what we *do* know. We *know* that our sexuality is God's good gift. We *know* that there are many ways in which people misuse God's good gift to abuse other people. We *know* that, as children of God, we must never hurt others by taking advantage of their sexual feelings or of what they do or do not know or understand about their sexuality. These things apply to all of us, regardless of our sexual orientation.

Remember Jesus' story of the Good Samaritan? A man was beaten by robbers and left to die. Two persons passed by. The first was a priest. The second was a Levite—a temple official. They weren't responsible for the problems of the man on the road, but just like the robbers, they also left him to die. It was a Samaritan—a person whom Jesus' listeners wouldn't have had anything to do with—who stopped and cared. Jesus used this story to explain the meaning of *neighbor* and to let us know that the neighbors we are called to love as we love ourselves are often people who are most unlike us (Luke 10:25-37).

Teenage Pregnancy

My older sister has a friend who is pregnant. She's only fifteen. Everybody seems worried about her. Why?

These are understandable worries. Teenagers might be *able* to have babies, but that ability doesn't mean that they are *ready* to do so. First of all, teenage girls are not *physically* ready for pregnancy and childbirth. Their babies are often underweight and frequently born prematurely—that is, before the end of a normal nine-month pregnancy. The death rate for premature babies born to teenage mothers is higher than the death rate for premature babies in general. Also, there are many instances where teenage mothers-to-be are either unable or unwilling to obtain proper **prenatal** (pree-NAY-tuhl) **care**—medical care for mothers and babies during pregnancy. This lack of care adds to the risks.

Teenagers are not *economically* ready to be parents. Teenaged parents often drop out of school. Their lack of education then makes it difficult for them to get good jobs. In many cases teenagers who become parents will face an entire lifetime struggling with money problems.

Teenagers are not *emotionally* ready to be parents. A child puts more pressure on young parents than their relationship can take. Few of these relationships last, and one parent—usually the mother—must take responsibility for raising the child alone.

Some young people believe that having a child will make them instant adults. Although becoming a teenaged parent pushes young people into adult responsibilities, it can't provide them with the adult maturity that is needed to handle those responsibilities. Teenagers who become parents cheat themselves out of the time they need to grow into adulthood naturally.

Many teenaged girls decide to terminate or end their pregnancy through **abortion** (uh-BORE-shun). Abortion is a surgical procedure. The menstrual lining and the embryo or fetus are drawn out of the uterus using a suction process. Abortion has been considered when pregnancy has threatened the life of the mother, when tests show that a fetus is seriously deformed, and when the pregnancy is the result of rape. Unfortunately, some people see abortion also as a means of birth control.

The decision to terminate a pregnancy is one that must be made with prayer and very careful thought. Some who choose abortion feel deep regret later on. A teenaged girl faced with this decision needs loving support. She needs to explore her feelings and consider how this decision is going to affect her now and later on. Parents, pastors, physicians, friends, and the father of the unborn child are important people to involve as the decision is made.

Some teenaged mothers place their babies up for adoption—another decision that requires a great deal of support. Enabling a childless couple to have a family and giving a child a better chance in life is a caring thing to do. Giving up a child is a very difficult thing to do.

While this statement is obvious, it needs to be said: Young people can avoid these problems with the decision not to be sexually active. The writer of Ecclesiastes helps with the reminder that God sets "the time for making love and the time for not making love" (3:5). For young bodies, minds, and lives, the time is not yet right.

Sex and Advertising

My mom gets really steamed over TV commercials that show kids being kind of sexy. She says commercials for jeans are the worst. What's the problem?

The problem is this: People are using sex and using *you* to make money. Producing television shows, radio programs, movies, newspapers, and magazines costs money. Some of the money comes from the advertisers—jeans manufacturers and others—who pay to have their products promoted. Some of the money comes from the consumers—the people who go to the movies, read the magazines, and buy the jeans and other products.

Think back once again to our discussion of stereotypes in chapter 3. People who are trying to sell their products create a stereotype—a picture of the ideal girl or boy. In convincing young persons that by seeing a movie or buying a product they will become this ideal girl or boy, advertisers stand to make a lot of money. Being sexually attractive is part of that ideal. How *you* feel about being a female or being a male is not the advertisers' concern. Their goal is to create the ideal then convince you that you can reach that ideal with their help.

Moms and dads and other concerned adults have a reason to get steamed. Young people like you are being taken advantage of. They realize how much you want to grow up and are aware that you are doing some serious thinking about what it means to be male and female. Advertisers are suggesting to you that you don't have to go through the long maturing process. If you use their product, you can be an adult *right now*! They're lying to you. No one cuts corners on the way to being all grown up. No one can sell you anything to make the growing faster.

I've read in the paper about the police arresting prostitutes. Why does someone become a prostitute?

Prostitutes are people—women, men, girls, and boys—who are paid to perform sexual acts. Persons who become prostitutes often have convinced themselves that there is no other way for them to earn the money that they need. Persons who set themselves up to be used by others—even when being paid for it—cannot feel good about themselves. Some prostitutes are looking for affection and love, but looking in the wrong places.

The lives of prostitutes are often filled with danger. They are frequently the victims of violence. Persons who pay to use a prostitute's body seldom care what happens to the prostitute. In many cities, local newspapers print the names of persons who have been arrested for trying to buy the services of prostitutes. In addition to the legal consequences, these persons often find their lives ruined by the publicity that their actions receive.

Being sexually active with many people puts prostitutes at greater risk for being infected with **Sexually Transmitted Diseases (STD's)**. Prostitution is illegal in most places. It is frequently associated with crimes of violence and drug use.

Sexual Abuse

Someone followed me on my way home from school. He started talking to me and acted real friendly. Then he touched me. I got scared and ran home. What did I do to make him bother me?

You did *nothing wrong*, but your question is one often asked by young people who have had similar experiences. They wonder what they have done to encourage such people. In most cases their only mistake was being in the wrong place at the wrong time.

Much attention has been given recently to the subject of **sexual abuse**. We are beginning to recognize how widespread the problem is. We have been telling girls and boys not to talk to strangers or to get into a car with someone they didn't know, but we didn't tell them *why*. So they wondered. We're doing a better job today. With boys and girls being more aware, hopefully the problem of sexual abuse will decrease.

Who are sex abusers? Sometimes they are strangers, but in most cases they are acquaintances—even friends and relatives. Most sex abusers are men, but women can be abusive as well. Because it is against the law to abuse a person sexually, sex abusers are persons who are guilty of a sexual crime.

Why do they abuse? It has to do, at least in part, with their confusion about sexuality. To *abuse* something is to use it in an improper or destructive way. That is what sex abusers do with sex. Many were abused as children, leaving them confused about the place of sex in their lives.

What do sex abusers *do*? Sometimes they touch a girl's breasts or vulva or a boy's penis. Some force their victims to undress and pose for photographs, to touch their genitals, or to have sexual intercourse with the abuser. The sexual abuse of a child is called **child molesting** (muh-LEST-ing). Forced sexual intercourse is called **rape**. Both girls and boys can be the victims of rape. The rapist is a male who forces his penis into the vagina, anus, or mouth of his victim; or a female who forces someone to perform a sexual act with her.

Some sex abusers give their victims alcohol or drugs in order to make them cooperate. Some will try to convince their victims that such acts are normal, that everyone is sexually active, or that the act is something that the victim really wants. Some say that performing such acts is a sign that a person is growing up or an expression of love. Some will even try to get a victim to believe that he or she *deserves* the abuse because of something the victim did in the past. If someone tries to convince you with a statement like these, don't believe it!

Some sex abusers physically overpower their victims. Some threaten to harm their victims or their victim's friends, family, pets, or home if they don't cooperate. Sex abusers often threaten the same harm if the victim tells anyone what has happened.

I love my dad, but he has done things that make me feel really strange. He comes into my bedroom at night and touches my breasts and my vulva. I pretend to be asleep. When he leaves, I lie awake and wonder what I've done to make him do this to me.

When the abuser and the victim are members of the same family, it is called **incest** (IN-sest). Incest is hard to understand. The victim wants the abuse to stop but is afraid of losing the love of the abuser. The victim might also worry about what will happen to the family if the abuse is reported. Sometimes abusive family members will use the possible break-up of the family as a threat to keep the victim quiet. Not only has the victim been cruelly abused, but he or she is also feeling guilty. Young people need the love of a family to help them with growing up. This makes it difficult to deal with something that could cause major conflict in the family.

Does this mean that we shouldn't let anyone touch us? I like it when my stepfather hugs me, so how is this wrong?

There's a big difference between loving hugs and kisses and being touched in inappropriate ways and on inappropriate parts of your body. For instance, when you have a cramp in your leg, your stepfather might be the best person to rub that cramp out. When you're upset, it may feel good to have his arms around you. The reason we mention incest here is because it does happen. Girls and boys who are victims of incest need to know that they are not to blame and need to know how to protect themselves.

The rule in *every* situation is *tell, tell, tell!* Do it *right away!* If the first person you tell doesn't listen or believe you, tell someone else. And keep telling until someone *does* listen and believe you. *Nobody* deserves to be abused. Victims of abuse frequently need medical attention. Girls who have begun menstruating and who are rape victims need *immediate* medical care in order to insure that pregnancy does not occur. The victims of any kind of sexual abuse need the support of persons who can help the victims through this frightening experience. When sexual abuse happens within families, everyone in the family will need help in understanding and getting over the abuse. The threats of abusers should be ignored. We have laws to protect the victims of abuse.

You don't have to worry every minute about being abused, but it's smart to be cautious. Avoid being alone in places where it would be difficult to get help if you needed it. Don't assume that all strangers are sex abusers, but be careful. Learn to listen carefully to what people are saying to you. The many excuses that persons give to convince young people to become sexually involved *don't* make sense.

Learn to listen to your *body*. It will often tell you that it's afraid before your mouth is able to say so. Trust your feelings. Understand your body and your sexuality. This understanding will help you to be aware of possible abuse

and to do something about it. Talk with others. A team effort can make you even safer.

Your body is your own. Your body and your sexuality are the gift of God. *No one has the right to abuse that gift.*

STD's and AIDS

I've been reading about kids who have AIDS. It scares me. What can you tell us about diseases people get from having sex?

You have every reason to be scared. These diseases scare *many* of us. We might not be at risk *personally*, but we live in a world where lots of persons *are* at risk—some of them are persons we know and care about.

When I was a little girl, Mother would often send me down to the basement to get something for her. I hated that basement—especially at night. At the bottom of the steps, right in the center of the basement floor, was a *big* furnace. Modern furnaces tend to be fairly small and not very scary. But that awful old thing was a *monster*—all dark and covered with big pipes that made it look like some horrible mutant octopus. When I had to go down in the basement, I'd stand at the top of the steps, take a huge breath, run down the steps, grab what I needed, and run back up before I needed to take another breath!

A couple of years ago, I visited that house, and the new owners invited me down into the basement to see a litter of puppies. The furnace and the basement weren't scary any more. If I had asked when I was a girl, maybe someone would have taken the time to explain the monster furnace to me. Maybe I wouldn't have been so afraid.

You *have* asked. Let's see what we can do to help you understand Sexually Transmitted Diseases (STD's) and **AIDS**.

STD's are passed from one person to another through sexual contact. Though STD is the more modern term, you may still hear these diseases called *VD* or *Venereal* (vuh-NEER-ee-uhl) Disease. There are more than twenty different STD's. Some of the diseases you might hear about are **syphilis** (SIF-uh-luhs), **gonorrhea** (gahn-uh-REE-uh), **chlamydia** (KLUH-mid-ee-uh), and **genital herpes** (HER-peez). Some STD's can be treated and cured. Others are not curable, meaning that people will have this disease for life and continue to be able to pass it to others.

The following symptoms are sometimes associated with STD's:

- Unusual discharges (leaking of a thick fluid) from the penis or vagina.
- Irritation, lumps, or sores in, on, or around the genitals.
- Pain or tenderness in the genitals, genital area, or abdomen.
- Painful urination or frequent need to urinate.

These symptoms do not automatically mean that a person has an STD. In fact, a person can have an STD and have no symptoms at all. These symptoms are also ones that can indicate the presence of other diseases—diseases that are not sexually transmitted. However, persons who are sexually active and have any of these symptoms are advised to see their doctor.

The germs that cause STD's need the proper conditions to survive—conditions such as those found in places like the penis, vulva, vagina, rectum, mouth, or throat. In order to pass the germ from one body to another, there must be direct contact of "STD survival places" between two persons. This kind of contact generally happens during sexual activity.

Most STD germs die soon after they leave the body and are exposed to the air. This fact makes it unusual for STD's to spread in ways other than human-to-human contact. Certain STD germs can be passed from an expectant mother to her unborn child and can cause a variety of birth defects in the child.

Responsible sexual behavior is the best prevention for STD's. For young people, responsible sexual behavior means waiting to become sexually active. For adults, responsible sexual behavior means a faithful commitment to one person.

AIDS stands for **Acquired Immune Deficiency Syndrome** (uh-KWIRED ih-MUNE duh-FISH-uhn-see SIN-drohm). The AIDS virus attacks the immune system of the body—the system that fights off disease. AIDS prevents the immune system from doing its job properly, making it something like an orchestra without a conductor. The body is unable to defend itself against diseases that it normally could fight off—pneumonia, for example—and some rare diseases that people with healthy immune systems seldom get.

The first cases of AIDS in the United States were recorded in 1981. Since then, thousands of deaths throughout the world have resulted from AIDS-related complications. The AIDS virus is most commonly spread by having sexual relations with someone who is infected. The sharing of needles and syringes by users of illegal drugs is the second most common way the AIDS virus is spread. The virus can also be passed from an infected mother to her baby before or during birth. It has also been spread to persons who have received transfusions of blood from donors who were infected with the AIDS virus. However, the procedures that are now used to test blood donations have just about eliminated the risk to people who receive blood.

The AIDS virus lives in blood, semen, and vaginal secretions. The virus may enter the body of anyone coming in contact with infected body fluids in one of the ways we have already mentioned. AIDS is not spread through casual contact. A boy or girl with AIDS who attends your school is not a threat to you. Using a toilet or a drinking fountain that has been used by someone with AIDS does not endanger you. Neither does playing sports or eating with someone who has AIDS.

Because AIDS symptoms may not appear until long after a person has been infected, it is not always possible to tell whether or not a person has AIDS. Therefore, the only way to be completely safe is the avoidance of all behavior that puts a person at risk. This includes the old ritual of becoming blood brothers or sisters. For years girls and boys have sealed their friendship by pricking their fingers and pressing it against the pricked finger of their friend—something that should be avoided.

At a workshop, a sixth grade boy came right out and asked me, "How can you be sure that the person you're having sex with doesn't have AIDS?" An honest question deserves an honest answer.

"You can't, I replied." And that's another reason why making good decisions about sex from the very beginning is so important."

He pushed me a step further. "What about a **condom** (KON-duhm)?"

Condoms are something like long, rolled up, oversized balloons. Before sexual contact happens, the man unrolls the condom over his erect penis. He must be careful to allow enough space at the end to catch the semen when he ejaculates, or the semen could be forced back up and out the open end. The condom prevents body fluids from coming into contact with each other. However, condoms can leak and they can tear during sexual activity, which means they are not 100% effective.

We protect ourselves by avoiding risky behavior. We avoid the use of illegal drugs and remain faithful to one sexual partner. We also reduce the threat of AIDS when we work at being honest and encourage others to do the same.

People's lives change. Some who have engaged in risky behavior eventually see their foolishness and receive forgiveness. The Bible tells the story of the woman caught committing adultery—having sexual intercourse with someone other than her husband—who was brought to Jesus. Those who brought her were ready to stone her to death for her sin. Jesus pointed out that they too were sinners and had no right to judge the woman. Jesus forgave her and said, "Go, but do not sin again" (John 8:1-11).

A person who has been exposed to AIDS may pass it on before developing AIDS symptoms. This means that persons must be honest with husbands, wives, or other sex partners about past risky behavior. That kind of honesty is seldom easy; but considering the tragedy of AIDS, it becomes necessary. One can be forgiven but cannot forget or try to hide the past.

Answering these questions has helped us to take a look at some of the issues that you face now or will face in the future. These are heavy issues for girls and boys your age, but knowing about these things will help you to make some of the big decisions related to your sexuality. In the next chapter, we'll think some more together about how those decisions are made.

Chapter 6

Responsible: Able to Respond

Have you ever become really frustrated while standing in front of your closet and trying to decide what to wear? In your mind you review where you're going, who's going to see you, and how they're going to react to what you have on. Maybe the color of your sweater or shirt is *not* an earth-shaking decision, but it's important to you. You put energy into making such decisions. Feeling tired after wrestling with choices is not unusual. Making decisions can be hard work.

Learning to Fly

Those who trust in the Lord for help
will find their strength renewed.
They will rise on wings like eagles;
they will run and not get weary;
they will walk and not grow weak.
Isaiah 40:31

The biblical writers were impressed with the size of the great eagles that glided and swooped above the mountains and valleys of Palestine. During a visit to the Holy Lands, our tour guide pointed out an eagle that seemed to be suspended in mid-air and told of a nest that perched on a cliff high above a deep ravine. Inside the nest a lone egg was being lovingly attended by a pair of eagles. When the time was right, a baby eaglet broke through the shell and entered the world as a living, breathing, creature of God. For weeks the eagles tended their baby, bringing food and standing protectively beside the nest.

Daily the eaglet grew stronger, stretching its back and neck in the warm sun and feeling the cool wind ruffle its feathers. It began to wonder about life in the eagle world of clouds and breezes, but it waited for the right moment to explore. The parent eagles also waited, watching for signs of readiness.

One day, the mother eagle knew that it was time. She flew to the nest. Instead of landing on the nest, she paused in mid air, fluttering and flapping her wings as if inviting the young eaglet to dance. Accepting her invitation, the eaglet moved from the nest onto her back, and together they explored the world of sky. At first she glided quietly, only moving her wings enough to catch the air currents. Suddenly she dove sharply toward the earth and then, almost teasingly, climbed upward once again. Clinging to its mother's back, the young eagle discovered the joy of flying.

The next day, the mother eagle returned and the events of the day before were repeated. Then, without warning, she flew as high as her strength would allow. With one sudden move, she flipped the eaglet off her back and into the air.

The startled eaglet began to fall. It struggled and flapped at the air, falling helplessly toward certain death. Circling close by, the mother eagle watched. Certain that her offspring could not fly on its own, she swooped beneath the eaglet, caught it on her wings, and returned it to the safety of the nest.

After a night of rest, the eaglet was coaxed once again onto its mother's wings. Again it was carried high above the ravine and allowed to fall. Again it flapped and fluttered frantically. At last the eaglet remembered what it had seen and what it had felt while riding on its mother's back. It moved its wings as it had seen its parents do, and its fall became flight. With pride the mother eagle watched. The eaglet soared through air and cloud, responding to the forces that pulled it down by catching the breeze and flying as God intends eagles to fly.

Soaring Like Eagles

Like the eagle, you live in a world of wonder—a world where there is much for you to discover. Your body and your mind are growing and changing. The changes *you* experience cause changes in the persons around you and in the relationships you have with those persons.

You are making more of your own decisions. Some are fairly simple ones like, "Shall I wear the red or blue shirt today?" or "Do I want an apple or a banana in my lunch sack?" Others are more difficult—truth telling, accepting responsibilities for duties at home, using home work time effectively, as well as decisions about relationships and about how you will express your sexuality.

Once your parents and other adults made most of your decisions for you. They also assumed the responsibility for what happened to you. When a child is injured, no one asks, "Why did Timmy run into the street?" Instead they demand, "Where were Timmy's parents?"

As you grow and mature, you are becoming increasingly self-reliant—you are learning to fly on your own. This means that your parents and the other adults who care for you take on different roles. As you need them to make fewer and fewer decisions for you, your relationship with them changes. This is one of the reasons why adolescence is a rather confusing time for some people. So much is changing all at once, it's hard to keep up with the changes.

You are using new skills and knowledge. You are becoming increasingly responsible for your own actions. You are making new acquaintances and new friends—folks beyond your immediate family circle—who are influencing the decisions you make. You are ready to ask, challenge, and debate with yourself and with others as you seek answers to your questions. You have many needs—the need to stretch yourself, the need to attempt new things, the need for adventure, and the need to understand yourself and others. You are trying to discover ways to have these needs met while recognizing that *others* have needs too.

Responsibility! What Does It Mean?

Each stage in life is important—including your passage from childhood into adolescence. With that passage you have new freedoms. With those freedoms come important challenges and responsibilities.

As an infant, your goal was to walk. You needed to get from one place to the other. With time and practice, you were able to respond to that need. Later you decided that you needed to get places faster, so you learned to run. As your world expands, you explore the boundaries of that new world. You are discovering needs and your new abilities to respond to those needs.

As a young child, you thought only of yourself. That is natural behavior for young children. Now you know you can't be that self-centered. You are responsible to others and responsible for others. You are able to respond—*response-able*. How do you begin to make all of the decisions that are required of a responsible person?

Faith and Five Smooth Stones

"Who's your favorite Old Testament character?" I asked a group of girls and boys. After a short discussion, their almost unanimous response was, "David!"

"Why do you like David?"

"Because David was so brave."

"Because David was loyal."

"Because David was just a kid like us when he fought Goliath!"

We pieced together and retold the story of David and Goliath. The story took place during a time of war. On one side of a great valley was camped the army of Saul, king of Israel. Across the valley was the army of the Philistines. For forty days, a Philistine named Goliath—a man reportedly over nine feet tall—challenged the Israelites day and night. "Choose one of your men to fight me. If he wins and kills me, we will be your slaves; but if I win and kill him, you will be our slaves. I *dare* you to pick someone to fight me!"

King Saul wasn't exactly swamped with volunteers. In fact, he didn't have *any* until David arrived. David had been home tending his father Jesse's sheep while some of his brothers fought in Saul's army. Anxious to find out how the battle was going, Jesse sent David to check on his brothers and then report back.

David heard Goliath's challenge and volunteered to fight the Philistine giant. Since it was Saul's only offer, he took David up on it. Refusing the armor and the weapons that Saul offered, David headed off to meet Goliath with the weapons of a shepherd—a stick and sling.

On his way across the valley, David crossed a stream. Reaching down into the water, he gathered up five smooth stones and put them into the bag that hung at his side.

Goliath laughed at David as they drew closer to one another. David said nothing. He reached into his bag, took out a stone, placed it in his sling, and began to swing it around and around his head. When David let the stone fly, he struck Goliath in the forehead, and the Philistine giant crashed to the ground.

How might you be like David? Think about this: Goliath was popular and powerful. *Your* Goliath—the giant that *you* have to face—might have something to do with your desire to be popular and powerful.

What was David's strength? It wasn't his size! David had two things going for him—two important lessons he had learned from his father. Jesse had shown David how to be a shepherd. Part of being a shepherd was learning how to protect the sheep. David knew how to choose his ammunition, he knew how to use his sling, and he knew where the stone from his sling had to hit.

The second lesson David learned from Jesse had to do with what was right and what was wrong. Jesse helped David understand the responsibilities that go along with being a child of God. David's strength was knowing that he was created by God and belonged to God. David knew that God would be with him—no matter how big the enemy. David felt good about himself as he went into battle with his weapons, his faith, and his five smooth stones.

Into the Conflict

Conflict is when we are being pulled in two directions and have to make a decision which way we will go. Conflict is not a bad thing. Without conflict, we'd never learn to make decisions.

We don't make our decisions all alone. When David decided to take Goliath on, he really wasn't alone. As he stooped to gather up the five smooth stones, David's family was with him. Like the eaglet learning to fly, David could rely on what he had experienced and what he had been taught at home to help him with his decisions. You can do the same thing. Your family goes with you into your conflicts. Families help form our values—the things that are important to us. When our values are clear, the decisions aren't as difficult and the conflicts aren't as frightening as they would be if we had no values.

David knew that there were stones in that stream that would help him and stones that wouldn't. As we go into conflict, we need to choose friends as carefully as David chose the stones for his sling. One key to our making wise choices is finding friends who will support us as we make our decisions. Friends are persons with whom we can have fun, share dreams, and talk about problems. We laugh with friends, shout with friends, and sometimes cry with friends. What kind of person do you want for a friend?

My guess is that you want someone you can trust. A friend is someone you can talk to, knowing that he or she will keep your confidence—breaking it only if your health and safety require it. You will want friends who are boys and friends who are girls. In order to make good decisions, it sometimes helps to talk to someone who is different from us—someone who sees a situation differently than we do. Boys are sometimes able to do this for girls, and girls for boys.

You will want friends who think about the results of their actions. A friend who endangers your safety, your health, or your happiness by offering you drugs or alcohol isn't much of a friend. Anyone who suggests that you experiment with sex before you're ready to deal with the consequences of your actions is *adding* conflict to your life, not helping you to *deal* with it.

What kind of friend do you want to be to others? You want to be someone they can respect, someone they can confide in, someone they can depend on. You want to be someone who supports them as they make choices. You want to be someone who demonstrates faith in God and love for friends by suggesting only things that will help your friends and your friendships to grow.

Think about the lessons you've learned from others—from those whose poor judgment brought grief to themselves and others and from those whose thoughtful actions were the source of joy. Trust your instincts. Listen to your conscience. Most of all—*think!* Don't rush into your decisions. Give the decision time. Give God time to speak to you and to help you understand God's will in that conflict situation. Your growing relationship with God is an important influence on your decision making abilities.

As you commit yourself to live as God's child, you learn that God provides you with great strength. When you know that God cares what is happening to you, you know you are never alone. God's truths, truths you never outgrow, are found in Scripture. You've always liked the story of David, but who would have thought that David and his sling shot would be a symbol of you and your life today? Those old stories remind us that we are God's children. They talk about real events and real feelings—birth and death, sorrow and joy, sadness and dance, tearing down and rebuilding, people moving farther apart and closer together. They talk about real conflicts and real decisions, reminding us that we *don't* go into our conflicts alone.

Decisions About Language

Throughout this book, we've talked about many of the decisions that you are making right now—decisions related to how you *understand* yourself and others and how you *feel* about yourself and others. One thing we haven't said much about is language. Girls and boys want to know what kind of language to use when they talk about their bodies and about their sexuality. They also are wondering about the dirty jokes that they hear.

When you get right down to it, words are just words. The issue is how we *use* those words. Words can be used to hurt, and words can be used to heal. Words can be used to build people up, and words can be used to bring people down. Some of the slang terms that refer to sexual intercourse are used to refer to hurtful and even violent actions. Is that the understanding of intercourse that we want to communicate to others?

Words scribbled on the walls of a public bathroom or sprayed on the side of a building aren't generally ones we are comfortable using around parents or other adults. It isn't that they wouldn't know these words. Chances are they would. Street language hasn't changed much over the years. It's object is to get a reaction from people. Language has power. Certain words can cause embarrassment and anger. Some people like to have the power to embarrass and anger others.

Some people are only able to talk about sexuality when they are joking about it. They can usually find an audience for their jokes so they get lots of practice and become comfortable with the jokes. They are uncomfortable using the *correct* words because they don't have a chance to practice using those words. I would encourage *you* to practice the proper terms until you become comfortable with them.

You have decisions to make about language and jokes. You'll discover with experience that some jokes are fun while others are unkind. You don't have all the answers now. You may never have them all. Ask yourself, *Does this story or word tear people down or humiliate me or others?* If so, you probably don't want to pass it on.

A Decision for Later: Family Planning

Yes, you are making more decisions all of the time, and an increasing number if those decisions will be related to your sexuality. This will continue through your adult years. People of *all* ages must make decisions about their sexuality.

Some couples choose not to have children or to limit the size of their families. Having made these choices, they have others to make. When they have sexual intercourse, they must decide about a method of **birth control**.

Birth control refers to any method used to prevent pregnancy. The object is to avoid conception—the fertilizing of the ovum by a sperm cell. The **birth control pill** contains hormones that cause a woman's body to act as though it is pregnant. As a result, no ova leave the ovaries. Without an ovum, there is no chance of pregnancy.

Some couples choose a **condom** (KON-duhm) which is placed over the erect penis of the husband. The condom holds the semen, preventing the sperm from reaching and fertilizing an ovum.

A **diaphragm** (DIE-uh-fram) is a kind of rubber cap, inserted into the vagina by the woman before having sexual intercourse. The diaphragm is usually used along with a **spermicide** (SPERM-uh-side). The diaphragm prevents sperm from entering the uterus and the spermicide destroys the sperm.

The **intrauterine** (in-tra-YOO-tuhr-in) **device** or **IUD** is a soft plastic or metal ring, coil, or loop that must be inserted into and removed from the uterus by a doctor. The presence of the IUD prevents the fertilized ovum from attaching to the lining of the uterus. Many doctors have questioned the safety of the IUD and hesitate to recommend it as a birth control method.

Natural Family Planning requires a couple to watch for signs of ovulation—such as the woman's body temperature. The couple then avoids sexual intercourse on those days when conception is possible.

Surgical methods of birth control are also possible. Couples who choose not to have children or not to have any *more* children may decide on either a **tubal ligation** (TOO-buhl lie-GAY-shun) or a **vasectomy** (vah-SEHK-tuh-me). A tubal ligation or "tying the tubes" is an operation where the woman's fallopian tubes are cut, tied, or sealed to prevent pregnancy from occurring. A vasectomy is an operation performed on the man which severs the vas deferens and prevents sperm from mixing with the semen. The ova continue to mature and leave the ovaries and the sperm continue to be produced in the testicles, but are absorbed by the body. Men continue to have normal ejaculations, but there are no sperm in the semen to cause fertilization. Doctors caution patients that they should consider these methods only if they are absolutely certain that they want to avoid pregnancy permanently.

Once again, I want you to think back to all that we have said about intimacy in past chapters. These are examples of major decisions that couples must make. It is important that they have talked them through together. The closer two people are, the easier it will be for them to make these and other big decisions.

Preparing for Decisions

Boys and girls your age will find it difficult to think ahead to when they'll be making decisions about having children. Ideally, these are choices you won't be making for quite some time. But we mention them for two reasons. The first reason is to provide you with information that will help to answer questions that you may have. The second reason is to give you examples of decisions that you can start preparing yourself *now* to make *later on*.

How do you prepare? Working at family relationships and building friendships are two very important ways. Decision making, as we have said, is hard work. It is also *lonely* work when you have to struggle with your conflicts all alone. What makes you better able to respond—more responsible? In part it's the example and the counsel of those who love you the most—your family and your friends.

You also prepare by working at your relationship with God. Paul's reminder to the Corinthians serves us as well:

"Surely you know that you are God's temple and that God's Spirit lives in you!" Paul continues, "God's temple is holy, and you are that temple" (1 Corinthians 3:16-17). *You are God's temple!* God couldn't be any closer. The temple is where God *lives*. God lives in you.

You are that temple, and you are holy. To be *holy* means to be wonderfully different—to be set apart for a special purpose. In one way or another, God's special purpose for you is to grow in body, in wisdom, and in your ability to love God and others.

These are not easy days for you. Everything is moving too slowly or too quickly. But there is strength in learning to wait for God's timing and to watch for God's purpose to be unfolded. You were created by God—male or female. You were created to create. Many decisions await you. With God's help, and with the help of your family and friends, you will be responsible—able to respond!

> Those who trust in the Lord for help
>   will find their strength renewed.
> They will rise on wings like eagles;
>   they will run and not get weary;
>   they will walk and not grow weak.
>   Isaiah 40:31

What a Fantastic Creation We Are!

1. This is the nose that sits here on my face; Two eyes and ears help to fill up the space;
2. Arms used for hug-ging and hands used to touch; Feet that like stomp-ing through pud-dles so much;
3. She bod-ies, he bod-ies: each one u-nique; Ev-'ry con-ceiv-a-ble size and phy-sique;
4. Some folks have bod-ies that don't work so well, Still they have stor-ies they can't wait to tell;

Two cheeks, one chin, and a mouth that can say How thank-ful I am God made me this way.___
God made a bod-y for you and for me. Let us take care of God's gift faith-ful-ly.___
Yours is the spe-cial one God had in mind. Look in the mir-ror and there you will find.___
If we just lis-ten we'll un-der-stand how we all fit in-to God's spe-cial plan now.___

O what a won-der-ful, mar-vel-ous, glor-i-ous, what a fan-tas-tic cre-a-tion we are!

When I look all a-round I am re-mind-ed we're far more a-maz-ing than earth, sea, and star.

WORDS AND MUSIC: James Ritchie
Copyright © 1984, 1987 by James Ritchie.

A Song to Celebrate Myself

*Autoharp markings are for the key of C.

WORDS AND MUSIC: Jerry O. Cook

Copyright © 1973 by Graded Press. Reprinted by permission of Jerry O. Cook.
Revised 1974; this arrangement copyright © 1986 by Graded Press.

Glossary

**The numbers at the end of the definitions direct you to the
pages where you will find more information about these terms.**

abortion (uh-BORE-shun). The surgical removal
of an embryo or fetus from a pregnant woman's
uterus before the embryo or fetus is able to survive
on its own. *82*

Acquired Immune Deficiency Syndrome (AIDS)
(uh-KWIRED ih-MUNE duh-FISH-uhn-see
SIN-drohm). A disease caused by the Human
Immunodeficiency Virus (HIV). AIDS causes the
breakdown of the body's immune system, making it
impossible for the body to fight off other diseases.
AIDS is transmitted by the exchange of body
fluids—primarily through sexual intercourse but also
through the sharing of needles by drug users and
from infected mothers to their babies. *88, 90*

adolescence (a-doh-LES-sens). The period between
childhood and adulthood. A young person going
through this period is referred to as an **adolescent**
(a-doh-LES-sent). *13*

amniocentesis (AM-nee-oh-sen-TEE-sis). The
surgical insertion of a hollow needle through a
woman's abdominal wall and into the uterus to
obtain a sample of the amniotic fluid. This process is
used to check for birth defects in a developing fetus.
65

amnion (AM-nee-ahn) or **amniotic sac**
(am-nee-AH-tik). The thin membrane sac filled with
a watery solution called amniotic fluid that
surrounds and protects the developing fetus in the
uterus. *65, 67*

ampulla (am-POOL-uh). The widened or
flared-out portion of the vas deferens near the
prostate gland, where sperm are stored until
ejaculated. *26, 28*

anus (AY-nuhs). The opening where solid waste
leaves the body. *24, 25*

athletic supporter. An elastic strap worn around
the pelvic area by men and boys during strenuous
exercise. Supports and protects the testicles by
holding them close to the body. Commonly known
as a jock strap. *28*

birth control. Preventing conception from taking
place. *102*

birth control pill. A medication taken exactly
according to the doctor's directions that prevents
ovulation and therefore prevents pregnancy. *102*

bisexuality. Being sexually active with or sexually
attracted to persons of both sexes. *80*

breach. When a baby is in something other than a
head-first position prior to birth. This position can
complicate the delivery, sometimes making a
caesarian section necessary. *68*

breasts. Two glands on the upper chest of both
males and females, the growth of which is stimulated
at puberty. In females, the breasts develop so that
they can produce milk at the birth of a baby. *32, 69*

caesarian section (sih-ZARE-ee-uhn). Delivery of
a baby by surgical incision through the abdomen
into the uterus. *67*

cervix (SIR-viks). The lower, narrow portion of the uterus which connects with the vagina. The cervix must open or widen in order to allow the baby to move into the vagina during birth. *66*

child molesting (muh-LEST-ing). The sexual abuse of a child. *85*

chromosomes (KROH-muh-sohms). Tiny rods in the nuclei of sperm and ova that carry the inherited factors from parents. The X and Y chromosomes determine the sex of the embryo. *65*

circumcision (sir-cum-SIZH-un). The surgical removal of the foreskin—the loose layer of skin that extends over the glans or head of the penis. One who receives this operation has been **circumcised** (SIR-cum-sized). *26, 27*

clitoris (KLIT-uh-ris). The small, cylinder-shaped, highly sensitive female organ located at the top of the inner labia. *23, 24*

conceive. To become pregnant.

conception (kuhn-SEP-shun). The fertilization of the female ovum by the male sperm, which marks the beginning of pregnancy. *57, 64*

condom (KON-duhm). A thin sheath, usually of rubber or latex, that looks like a long, rolled up, oversized balloon. It is placed on the erect penis before sexual intercourse to prevent the spread of disease and/or to prevent pregnancy. *91, 102*

contractions (kuhn-TRACK-shuns). The sudden shortening of the muscles in the uterus that push the baby into the vagina and out of the mother's body. *66*

delivery. The baby leaving the mother's body. *67*

diaphragm (DIE-uh-fram). A soft rubber dome or cap that is filled with a spermicide and inserted into the vagina before sexual intercourse to prevent pregnancy. *102*

dilate (DIE-late). The opening or widening of the cervix to allow for the vaginal delivery of a baby. *67*

ejaculation (ee-jack-yoo-LAY-shun). The release or squirting of semen from the penis caused by the strong squeezing of muscles and the prostate gland during orgasm. *28, 37*

embryo (EM-bree-oh). An unborn human from about the tenth day after conception until the third month of pregnancy. *66*

epididymis (ep-uh-DID-uh-mis). A mass of tiny tubes attached to the back of each testicle; the sperm cells mature as they move through the tubes. *26, 28*

erection (ee-RECK-shun). The enlargement and hardening of the penis as sexual stimulation causes blood to rush to the genital area, filling tiny hollow sacs inside the shaft. Muscles at the base of the penis tighten and prevent the blood from flowing out of the penis. Females experience the erection of the clitoris in response to sexual stimulation. *26, 31, 35*

estrogen (ESS-truh-juhn). The female sex hormone that is produced primarily in the ovaries and is responsible for the development of secondary sex characteristics such as breast development and widened hips. *31*

fallopian (fa-LOH-pee-uhn) **tubes**. The two tubes that branch out from either side of the upper part of the uterus, through which the ova pass from the ovaries to the uterus. *24, 25*

feminine (FEHM-uh-nin). Qualities associated with being female. **Femininity** (fehm-uh-NIN-uh-tee) is how a person expresses her understanding of what it means to be female. *54*

fertilization (fer-tuhl-uh-ZAY-shun). The union of the sperm cell nucleus with the nucleus of the ovum to start a new baby. Also called **conception**. *65*

fetus (FEE-tuhs). An unborn human from about the third month of pregnancy until birth. *66*

foreplay (FOR-play). Sex play that precedes and prepares persons for sexual intercourse. *63*

foreskin (FOR-skin). The loose layer of skin that covers the glans or head of a male's penis at birth. Its removal is called **circumcision**. *25*

fraternal. A multiple birth that began with the release of more than one ovum and the fertilization of those ova by different sperm. *68*

gay. A homosexual person; more specifically, a male homosexual. *80*

gender. Being male or female. *17*

genes. The part of every body cell that carries information about characteristics that one inherits from either or both parents. *29*

genitals (JEN-uh-tuhls) or **genitalia** (jen-uh-TAIL-yuh). The external male and female sex organs—the penis, scrotum, and testicles in males, and the vulva in females. *23*

heterosexuality (HET-uh-roh-sek-shoo-AL-uh-tee). Being sexually active with or sexually attracted to persons of the other sex. *80*

homosexuality. Being sexually active with or sexually attracted to persons of one's own sex. *60, 80*

hormones (HOR-mohns). Chemical substances, produced by glands, that regulate the functioning of other organs. *25*

hymen (HI-muhn). A thin layer of tissue that partially covers the opening to the vagina. It may be torn during athletic activity or stretching movement, or during first sexual intercourse. Some women are born without a hymen. *23, 24*

identical. A multiple birth that began with the complete division of the fertilized ovum, forming two or more babies that are completely alike. *68*

incest (IN-sest). Sexual intercourse between close relatives; a practice forbidden in most cultures. *86*

intercourse. See *sexual intercourse*.

intimacy. (IN-tuh-muh-see). The process of building close relationships between people through getting to know and learning to accept one another. *47, 70*

Intrauterine Device (IUD) (in-tra-YOO-tuhr-in). A soft plastic birth control device that must be inserted into and removed from the uterus by a doctor. Many questions have been raised as to the safety of this means of birth control. *102*

labia (LAY-bee-uh). Two sets of folds of skin that are part of the vulva. The outer or major labia surround the opening to the vagina. The inner or minor labia are inside and sometimes hidden by the outer labia. The word *labia* means "lips." *23*

labor. The stage of giving birth during which the cervix dilates or opens up, allowing the contractions of the uterine muscles to push the baby from the uterus into the vagina in preparation for delivery. *66*

lesbian (LEZ-bee-uhn). A female homosexual. *80*

masculine (MASS-kyuh-lin). Qualities associated with being male. **Masculinity** (mass-kyuh-LIHN-uh-tee) is how a person expresses his understanding of what it means to be male. *54*

masturbation (mass-ter-BAY-shun). The deliberate touching or stroking of the genitals to create sexual pleasure. *31, 37, 58*

menopause (MEHN-uh-pahz). The time in a woman's life—usually between the ages of 45 and 55—during which menstruation ceases and pregnancy is no longer possible.

menstruation (men-STRAY-shun). The discharge of blood, secretions, and tissue from the uterus that females experience for from four to seven days, about once a month. The entire process is called the **menstrual** (MEN-struhl) **cycle**. The time during which the discharge takes place is called the **menstrual period** or simply the **period**. *32-34*

miscarriage (miss-KAIR-ihj). When an embryo or fetus is expelled from the uterus before it is mature enough to survive, usually due to some abnormal development. More properly referred to as a spontaneous abortion.

morning sickness. The upset stomach that some pregnant women experience, particularly during the first three months of pregnancy. It is so named because it often takes place in the morning. *69*

Natural Family Planning (NFP). Women wanting to avoid pregnancy keep charts of such things as daily body temperature in order to tell when ovulation is to take place. Intercourse is then avoided on days when conception is possible. *102*

nocturnal emission (nock-TER-nal ee-MISH-uhn). The ejaculation of built-up semen that occurs during sleep and is often associated with sexual dreams. Also called a **seminal emission** or **wet dream**. *37*

orgasm (OR-gaz-uhm). The intense and pleasant pulsing of muscles that signals the highest point of excitement in sexual activity. *31, 63*

ovaries (OH-vuh-reez). Two almond-sized female reproductive glands in which ova develop and sex hormones are produced. *24, 25*

ovulation (ah-vue-LAY-shun). The ripening and release of an ovum from an ovary, occurring about once a month. *32*

ovum (OH-vuhm). The female reproductive cell. The plural is **ova** (OH-vuh). *25, 32*

penis (PEE-nuhs). The cylinder-shaped part of the male genitals through which urine and semen pass. The cylinder part is the **shaft**; the very sensitive end or head is the **glans** (GLANZ). *25, 26*

period. See *menstruation*.

pituitary gland (pih-TOO-uh-tare-ee). An endocrine gland attached to the base of the brain which secretes a number of hormones to control body processes. *30*

placenta (pluh-SEN-tuh). A spongy organ containing a network of blood vessels that develops on the lining of the uterus during pregnancy; it enables the exchange of food, oxygen, and waste materials between mother and child. *32*

pregnancy (PREG-nun-see). The period from conception to birth. The condition of having a developing embryo or fetus within the female body. *25*

prenatal care (pree-NAY-tuhl). Medical care for mothers and babies during pregnancy. *81-82*

prostate gland (PROSS-tate). An organ surrounding the male urethra that secretes part of the seminal fluid. The squeezing action of the prostate helps to force the semen out through the urethra during ejaculation. *26, 28*

prostitute (PROSS-tuh-toot). A person who is paid to perform sexual acts. *84*

puberty (PEW-bur-tee). The period when the body changes from that of a child to that of an adult; the sex organs mature and begin to produce mature ova or sperm. *29*

pubic hair (PEW-bick). Coarse, curly hair that grows in the genital area. *31*

rape. Forcing someone to have sexual intercourse. *85*

rectum. The lower end of the large intestine, ending at the anus. *24*

sanitary napkin. A pad of absorbent cotten worn inside the underpants to absorb the menstrual discharge. *33*

scrotum (SKRO-tum). The pouch of skin, beneath the penis, that contains the testicles. *26, 27*

semen (SEE-muhn). The whitish fluid ejaculated from the penis during orgasm. Also called **seminal fluid**. *28*

seminal vesicles (SEM-uh-nuhl VESS-ih-kuhls). Two small pouches located at the back of the male prostate gland, where semen is produced. *26, 28*

sexual abuse. When one person uses sexual actions or sexual language to hurt, frighten, embarrass, or take advantage of another person. *85*

sexual intercourse. Sexual activity where the penis is inserted into the vagina. *25, 63, 70*

sexuality. The sum of a person's sexual orientation, characteristics, and behaviors.

Sexually Transmitted Diseases (STD's). A variety of diseases that are passed from one person to another through sexual activity. These were formerly called Veneral Disease or VD. Some examples are **syphilis** (SIF-uh-luhs), **gonorrhea** (gahn-uh-REE-uh), **chlamydia** (KLUH-mid-ee-uh), and **genital herpes** (HER-peez). *84, 88-89*

sperm. The male reproductive cells produced in the testicles. *27*

spermicide (SPERM-uh-side). A sperm-killing chemical placed in the vagina prior to sexual intercourse. *102*

stereotype (STAIR-ee-oh-type). An image that suggests what all people within a group are or ought to be like. Stereotypes do not recognize the individuality of each person. *48*

sterilization. The surgical process of making a person permanently incapable of reproduction. *102-103*

tampon (TAM-pahn). A roll of absorbent material that is inserted into the vagina to absorb the menstrual discharge. *33*

testicles (TESS-tih-kuhls) or **testes** (TESS-tees). The egg-shaped male reproductive glands in which sperm and testosterone are produced. They are suspended in a loose pouch of skin between the legs. *26, 27*

testosterone (tess-TOSS-tuh-roan). The male sex hormone, produced primarily in the testicles, which is responsible for the full development of the genitals and sex characteristics such as hair growth and muscle development. *34*

tubal ligation (TOO-buhl lie-GAY-shun). A surgical procedure for sterilization in females. The fallopian tubes are cut, tied, sealed, or otherwise blocked off, either through an incision in the abdomen or through the vagina. Ova continue to be produced but they are reabsorbed by the body. *102*

umbilical cord (uhm-BILL-uh-kuhl). The cord connecting the unborn infant to the placenta through which the fetus receives nourishment and gets rid of waste materials. *66*

urethra (yoo-REE-thruh). The narrow tube through which urine passes out of the body from the bladder. In females, the urethra is totally separate from the vagina. In males, the urethra is also a part of the reproductive system, serving as a passageway for semen. *23, 24, 26*

uterus (YOO-ter-us). The muscular, hollow organ in females, shaped like a lightbulb or upside-down pear, in which babies grow and are nourished before birth. Also called the **womb** (WOOM). *24, 25*

vagina (vuh-JIE-nuh). An elastic, muscular passage leading from the uterus to the outside of the body. Receives the erect penis during sexual intercourse and allows a baby to pass from the womb and out of the mother's body during delivery. Also referred to as the birth canal. *23, 24, 25*

vas deferens (VAZ DEHF-uhr-uhnz). The tube in the male through which sperm passes from the epididymis to the seminal vesicles and urethra. Also called the **spermatic duct**, **sperm duct**, or simply the **vas**. *26, 28*

vasectomy (vah-SEHK-tuh-me). The surgical procedure for sterilization in males. On both sides of the scrotum, a small incision is made and the vas deferens is cut, tied, sealed, or otherwise blocked off. Normal ejaculation of semen continues, but the semen no longer contains sperm. Sperm continue to be produced but they are reabsorbed by the body. *102*

virgin. A person who has not experienced sexual intercourse. *72*

vulva (VUL-vuh). The external sex organ of the female. Includes the labia, clitoris, and the openings to the vagina and urethra. *23, 24*

vulnerability (vuhl-ner-uh-BILL-uh-tee). A weakness or an obstacle one cannot overcome. Vulnerabilities mean that we must often depend on the help of others. *47*